WHY STRATEGIC PLANNING DOESN'T WORK

WHY STRATEGIC PLANNING DOESN'T WORK

and

HOW TO MAKE SURE YOURS DOES!

The Methodology For High-Level Course-Plotting

A Workbook

Charles E. Cherry
Managing Partner
ADG Strategy Catalyzation

KEYMON BOOKS

New York   Huntersville

KEYMON BOOKS
9911 Rose Commons Drive, Suite E
Huntersville, NC 28078
keymonbooks@att.net

ISBN: ISBN-13   978-1479394852

Printed in the United States of America

"Operational excellence takes care of the present; only strategic realization takes care of the future!"

CONTENTS

PART I   INITIATING THE METHOLOGY

SECTION ONE:

The Preliminaries

SECTION TWO:

Determining Where The Company Stands Now

SECTION THREE:

Establishing The Company's Ambitions

PART II   COMPLETING PLAN GENERATION

HOW THE COMPANY IS TO REALIZE ITS AMBITIONS

INTERSESSION

PLAN COMPLETION

PART III   EXECUTING THE STRATEGIC PLAN

PART IV   THE ANNUAL UPDATE

APPENDIX

Introduction

"Every man has a plan that will not work."

How do you stop incest?

That is, in plotting course for the company, how do you eliminate the introversions of company habit, company bias, company preconception, company predisposition?

Virtually every company attempts – or pretends to honor – strategic planning. Too often the effort is a poorly-conceived waste of time better spent with customers. The result is a business landscape littered with tomes, sometimes ponderous, purporting to be strategic plans. The documents rarely are read, and even less referred to. In their formation, bright young managers, obliged to participate in fruitless exercises, are heard to say, "Let me get rid of this crap so I can get back to my job!"

It comes down to this: unless management teams can differentiate between genuine strategic engagement and mere extended operational planning, unless rote exercise can be avoided, unless the ability to conceive can be stretched, unless there is willingness truly to embrace change – the company is unlikely to be able to make magnitude leaps.

Real-world chief executives and managers don't need academic disquisition on the merits and wonders of strategic planning. They don't need theory. They don't need philosophical speculation. They don't need, either, "retreats" to the mountains where they will have nothing to do but seek inspiration to magic strategies. Such exercises indeed *are* "retreats" – from the real world and the pain of confronting reality. What managements do need is a sure footed way of developing superior strategic plans whose mettle will be proven in meaningful, visible, measurable, performance results.

That is the purpose of this workbook. Not to expound the academic, not to regale with war stories, not to parade, except incidentally, examples – which never will be useful – of what other companies have done. Instead, there is laid out here the 1-2-3 of how to formulate and execute a strategic plan that will work. There are no lengthy discourses, no expounding of esoteric notions, only set-by-step how to get the job done - on your own.

Can you do it yourself? It depends. If the management team is smart enough to understand a quite straightforward underlying logic, and *has the discipline* to carry through the dictates of the formulation it creates, it can. If it possesses neither ability, it is commended to the care and feeding of a professional practitioner.

In over twenty years of guiding the strategic planning of companies, or segments of companies – great and small, privately held and Big Board listed, in high-tech and basic products, industrial and consumer, manufacturing and services – the author rarely has come upon any who had not already in one form or another been pursuing plotting, if only by the seat of the pants of the CEO. But all of the organizations had in common dissatisfaction with the effectiveness of the way they were doing it. The aim, then, is to strip away illusion and superfluity, and for those who believe they are capable of do-it-yourself application, to instruct exactly in proven methodology.

CEC
October 2012

THE GUTS OF STRATEGIC PLANNING

Strategic planning can be stated simply and accurately as determining succinctly:

1. WHERE WE ARE

2. WHERE WE WANT TO GO

3. HOW WE'RE GOING TO GET THERE

Easy as pie, isn't it?

Right. Conceptually.

The actual doing, however, can be daunting. An effort could be a floundering exercise to no meaningful result. The purpose of this guide is to prevent that.

WHY STRATEGIC PLANNING DOESN'T WORK

This and the following section are to establish the mind-set necessary before initiating strategic planning

▶ *An inordinate number of chief executives are dissatisfied with the effectiveness of plotting course in their companies, then executing the plan.*

Why is this so?

Strategic planning either makes things happen in a clearly apparent, dramatic way, or it's a failure. When the pursuit fails, the roots are in one, more, or all of the following:

1. It's *hard* to do!

2. A genuine strategic mind-set is never attained.

3. The right questions are not posed.

4. It's done in dribs and drabs, by the wrong people, often as a rote exercise, with only lip service paid to carrying out the dictates developed.

5. Confrontation of the unfavorable, the unpalatable, and the difficult is diluted or evaded altogether.

6. There is inadequate stretching of the powers to conceive.

7. There is confusion between operational decision- making

and strategic planning, or between strategic planning and long-range planning.

8. It proceeds from an inside-out, rather than outside-in viewpoint (the customer's, that is!).

9. Unity of purpose is never achieved

10. Free expression is inhibited, thus hidden gold is mined.

11. There's neither belief nor commitment, nor reason for commitment.

12. Terror of embracing change is an insidious restraint.

13. The mechanism for driving execution is faulty.

14. Achievement against strategic plan is *not* a basis for performance measurement

15. At one extreme, there is paralysis by analysis or, at the other, there is intellectual puerility.

All organizations must continuously attend to day-to-day operations and how constantly to improve equipment, staffing, sales and marketing approach, the minutia of administration and all the rest, but this is NOT strategic planning. Strategic planning is directed at bringing about substantial CHANGES in magnitude, in revenue, in profitability, in products offered, in markets served, even to the extent of entry into an entirely different business. Long-range planning, on the other hand, is concerned with issues of staffing, space, equipment, location and financing when business results in the future have already been posited. Utility companies, e.g., plan how to accommodate demand in relation to population increases.

ASSURING _YOUR_ STRATEGIC PLAN DOES WORK

Start with clear understanding:

Strategy equates to gaining competitive advantage. No other definition is meaningful. Your company exists in a universe of itself, potential customers, and competitors. If you did not have competition, you do not need strategy. Strategic planning, then, intrinsically is directed to altering strengths relative to the competition, - but, ANOTHER CAUTION, *this has to be in terms* of _meaning to the customer_.

DON'T EVEN THINK ABOUT IT UNLESS FOUR ESSENTIALS ARE OPERATIVE

These are:

- **A Methodology** - you must follow an ordered approach by which plan integrity is assured.

> The methodology here is **high-end plotting.** Allusion was made in the introduction to "mountain retreat" planning which is too prone to be escape and casual speculation. Ordinary planning exercises may employ some of the basic principles of planning, but there is no short cut to the satisfaction only thorough, demanding effort can achieve.

- **Reach** - you must draw on all the imagination, innovation, ingenuity, creativity, stretch, boldness and courage of which the planning team is capable. Otherwise you likely are doing operational, not strategic, planning.

- **Discipline** - out front, you must be willing to exercise strict, ongoing adherence to the precepts of the plan.

- **The Horses** - you must have in place, or be able to put in place, the people and resources it takes to execute or the planning process is an exercise in fantasy.

The First Decision

Before anything else can be attempted the company has to confirm what its fundamental driving force has been in the past and decide what the choice is to be for the future. For some companies identification of what the force has been is easy to arrive at; for others it is less clear whether the company, in contrast to first supposition, has in fact been driven by market, by product, by technology, by method of sale or distribution, or by other impellent. Whatever the case, the basic determination to be made is: should the company continue to be driven as it has in the past, or should the fundamental force be different in the future?

Only A Very Few Underlying Strategies Are Possible

While numerous "strategies" can be conceived in support of how a company is to realize its goals, there are only a limited number of basic strategies. These are:

- **Exploiting areas of possibility**

- **Leveraging an existing advantage**

- **Intensifying a prime success factor**

- **Radicalization of established practice**

  - plus: two shadow strategies, so called because they are not strategies in themselves but last-resort responses to the inexorable, i.e.:

- **Entering an entirely new business**

- **Liquidation**

Avoiding Black Holes

Strategic planning is a vain effort unless the company:

- *genuinely* wants to make magnitude leaps

- *will* embrace a vision of itself

- develops reliable market scenarios

- constructs adept product/market analyses from which all courses flow, as opposed to simplistic sketching

- understands what differentiations it might essay in the market place, and which are achievable and which not

- is scrupulously objective in evaluating competitors

- can distinguish between what customers apparently want and what they really want

- can detail exactly the steps necessary to achieve the goals established

- avoids doing the same thing, in the same way, on the same battleground as the competition

- eliminates reliance on reputation and past successes

- eschews *rah, rah* as a substitute for focused attack

Conversion To Action

The essence of strategy formulation is conceptualization, but conceiving is only the starting point. Realization of strategy depends on the development of thoroughly worked-out action plans, which are truly strategic in nature - that is, demonstrate forcefully the likelihood of securing competitive edge - and to which genuine commitment has been made. The challenge of the strategic planning process is to establish a body of plans that makes rational promise, has high credibility, is sufficient to the purpose, and engenders confidence that the effect intended will come about. Executing the body and its components afterward, of course, is far more demanding still!

The Obstacles

The impediments standing in the way of companies pursuing strategic planning are formidable because:

- company planning teams cannot bring to bear the dispassion and independence of thought it takes to obviate biases, cherished ideas, sacred cows and preconceptions.

- they are unable to rid themselves of smugness, conceit and comfort with the status quo.

- they cannot overcome the hurdles of honest divergences of opinion, personality differences, playing off the boss (or others), and, in some cases, personal agendas out of synch with company vision.

- they have a functional blindness to their defects. They are suffering not because they cannot solve their problems but because they cannot <u>see</u> them.

- the individuals know each other too well.

- they have not learned the specific expertise and techniques necessary to enable results-producing strategic planning.

- they cannot generate the fresh ideas, the invention, the imagination, the innovation, integral to distinguished strategic planning.

  At the start of a planning process, participants typically fall into three categories:

  - those who are enthusiastic about the process

  - those who are uncertain

  - those who are resistant

Companies are challenged to make group dynamics operative in a way that influences positively drawing out full and equal participation by all planning team members, so that there is neither domination by articulate, but not necessarily soundest-thinking participants, nor hanging back by the less vocal who often have important contribution to make.

Finally, even after the imperative for strategic planning is accepted, companies stall and wiggle and evade getting at embrace of the discipline and the ongoing stringency required.

Why The Organization *Must* Embrace Strategic Planning

☐ To make things happen.

☐ To assure the future, - when around the company much is changing – things it knows about, things it does not.

☐ To thwart competitors who right now are conjuring ways to steamroller you.

☐ To heed the prickings of ambition.

☐ To shake up the status quo.

☐ To enable more adroit negotiation of the greased poles arrayed on the playing competitive playing field.

☐ To accelerate progress.

☐ To detail how the company is to achieve its vision. If it can't prescribe the path to follow, it *cannot* realize the vision.

☐ To realize fully potentials it clearly has, and uncover those it may be unaware exist.

☐ To overcome the destructiveness of comfort and resistance to change.

☐ To annul influences for decline, and their counterpart: floating in the wind.

☐ To instill unity of purpose, to motivate, to embed a sense of direction.

PART I

INITIATING THE METHODOLOGY

SECTION ONE

The Preliminaries

Embracing The Methodology

"Everyone talks about the weather but nobody does anything about it."

The logic of strategic planning is straightforward: where you are, where you want to go, how you're going to get there. The intellectual appreciation never gets more complicated than that. The practical mounting of each of the three steps, however is challenging, at times to the point of utter confoundment. The approach and techniques described in the next section - the how-to - were derived from extensive experience across a wide range of business circumstances, practiced analysis of the ingredients necessary for results-producing plans, and a particular sense of the imperatives.

Commonly, a company may have some kind of strategic plan in place: visible or invisible, rudimentary or sophisticated, operative or inoperative. Whatever the situation, the process set forth here incidentally will serve as a cross-check on the existing. Some companies will find gratification in the comparison; others may discover cause for dismay. To all shadings, however, it will become apparent that their best interest lies in strict adherence to the prescription. The logic of the methodology will quickly be comprehended. So will the interlocking of all the elements, though appreciation of that may take a bit longer.

The pursuit of strategic planning can never be a rote exercise, but the basic principles are to be observed whatever the peculiar needs of the organization. A prime acceptance must be made that the methodology presented here is sound and that it will be followed slavishly. The method was not developed by theory, but empirically, from long experience in what works and what does not. The temptation might be to attempt short-cuts and introduce wrinkles but, once adulteration is introduced, the integrity – and efficacy - of the process is threatened and the chances of success are reduced, or may be obviated entirely. Strong admonishment is made, then, to stick to the logic and the precepts. If that is done and good results are not obtained the author will personally refund you the price of this book

Selecting The Planning Team

The prime responsibility of the chief executive is strategic planning. The obligation _**cannot be delegated**_. The wise chief executive, however, realizes that great advantage, to the point of necessity to exploit it, lies in usage of the collective talents of the best in the organization. It is a team of the possessors of these talents that he recruits and says to it, "Help me do my job. Help me carry out my prime responsibility, because the sum of the brains in the planning room surely will be greater than mine alone."

The planning team consists of the chief executive of the company or business unit, (whatever the individual's title), the key functional managers reporting to him or her, plus selected non-reporters who are estimated likely to be strong contributors. It should not need to be said that STRATEGIC PLANNING CANNOT BE PURSUED WITHOUT THE INTIMATE PERSONAL INVOLVEMENT OF "THE BOSS". If the chief executive does not subscribe to the art, he or she does not understand that strategic planning is the chief responsibility of the office, and a question is immediately raised as to why the individual is in the position.

The same applies to managers who would seem logically to be placed on the team by reason of the position they hold, but if they are unlikely to be positive, diligent contributors, invitation to participate should be extended.

There is no ideal number for the planning team. For a start-up – yes, start-ups *better* do their strategic planning before they do anything else! – a team of three, perhaps the entrepreneur, a business manager kind, and a representative of the venture capitalist, might be completely adequate. For companies of substantial size teams on the order of nine to twelve in number are typical. No matter how large the company, however, to go much beyond a dozen participants is very likely to make the team unwieldly and a hindrance to focused creation. Eventually virtually everyone in the organization will have an assigned a role in executing the plan's dictates, so it is not critical that every possible worthy individual be included in the early process.

The chief executive, then, selects the team. He or she will, of course, especially in larger companies, encourage nominations from among the management group to assure that a high potential candidate for inclusion has not been missed.

A representative team might be: president, vice-president of sales, marketing director, manufacturing manager, director of engineering, special projects manager, chief financial officer, international markets manager, manager of human resources. In any company the composition should be whatever is most apt.

Choosing The Process Leader

The process is guided by a leader. Does he or she have to be a worker of magic? Yes! How does a plan leader become a magician? By following meticulously the methodology. There will be times during the high-level proceedings when it may not be crystal clear where it is headed. It is at the end of rigorous adherence to the prescription that the rainbow appears, sometimes to the amazement of the very individuals who have produced the plan, some of whom will bow to the necromancy the leader has worked.

The task of the leader is entirely *to insure the integrity of the process.* The assignment does not carry direct responsibility for the content of the plan, only that the methodology for producing it is meticulously adhered to. Logic in, logic out! Faulty adherence will produce faulty results. It is the team as the whole which bears the burden of achieving qualitative excellence in the output of the process

Anyone can be the facilitator! Well, almost. The single exception is the chief executive, who is unacceptable for two reasons:

1. The holder of that position cannot avoid dominating the process if he or she were to lead it. The boss is the boss and, no matter how stringent the effort to avoid the trap, people cannot help playing off the boss. In the planning process the chief executive is a member of the team, not its facilitator, though, of course, in execution of the plan the individual's overall leadership role will be asserted.

2. An aspect of the value of the process is to give the chief executive opportunity to observe how individual team members perform, make contribution and measure up. It is not possible to be a keen observer and director of the process at the same time.

To continue, when saying that anyone can be the facilitator it means that the individual can come from within or without the company but must bring these assets:

• after studying the process as here laid out, a thorough understanding of the methodology.

• capability of independence, dispassion and objectivity. If the chief executive has the courage and commitment to empower even a lower level manager who has these abilities, such an individual can serve admirably. Otherwise, an operating manager from an outside company who is known to have smarts and the appropriate temperament is an excellent candidate, as is an academic from a near business school – with proviso that the individual also does have practical management experience and can eschew personal biases on how strategic planning should be pursued. Lawyers can also be excellent candidates from their experience in disputation and advocacy.

- ability in group dynamics

- ability circumspectly to challenge

- a talent for stimulation

In whatever way the person is selected, the process leader, in acting as prompter and enforcer, is reinforced in the office by the chief executive as the leader:

- puts the planning team on ordered course and keeps it there

- assures that the crucial issues are identified

- prompts the asking of the hard questions

- separates the meaningful from the inconsequential

- employs diplomacy in conflict resolution

- encourages creativity

- orchestrates the complexities of the process and the diversity of the participants

- goads, tortures, inspires, cajoles, reinforces, opens eyes

- evaluates critically

- plays devil's advocate

- draws out full contribution by each player

- denies mediocrity

- urges the organization to work its own magic

If plea is made that no such paragon can be identified, the response is: Nonsense! Be more diligent in the search! Good people rise to the occasion once an assignment is clearly defined. The concepts driving the planning methodology are quite easy to understand and apply – that's why they work. It's the discipline to be adhered to that is the most challenging element in the process. To foster this rigor is the charge to the process leader.

BUT … if, in the judgment of the chief executive and the planning team indeed no individual on the organization's payroll can be considered for the appointment, the resort is to either of:

1. Identifying and inviting a member* of the business faculty of a nearby (or distant, for that matter) university, to serve as the process leader.

> *a member, that is, who, after interview and indoctrination in the methodology rigorously to be employed, is deemed to have the requisite qualifications just enunciated.*

-or

2. Engaging a professional facilitator, similarly interviewed and qualified.

Establishing The Product/Market Matrix

The entire future of a company is defined by its plotting of its products offered against markets served, in four quadrants so:

► Present goods or services offered to present markets

► Present goods or services that could be offered to new markets

► New goods or services possibilities that could be offered to present markets

► New goods or services possibilities that could be offered to new markets

No other possibilities exist. Agreed?

If, then, the four quadrants describing product offerings are laid out on a grid, for which a model follows on the next page, the entire universe of the company as planning starts becomes graphically visible. What it will look like when the strategic plan is put in place may be quite different. In any case, the grid must be prepared as the penultimate step prior to beginning actual planning.

The starting grid may be constructed by any knowledgeable, fully-informed individual within the company, who hands off the completed grid to the process leader (if the leader is a different individual) and the chief executive for confirmation of its accuracy, following which it is distributed to all team members for reference in the course of actual planning.

Obviously the number of product/market "boxes" a particular company might mark on the grid could be few or very many. Almost never would the four quadrants be equal. "Product" can often be shown as a product line rather than an individual item. For the purposes of strategic planning only certain of the boxes will come under scrutiny but, over time, obviously every box must be analyzed by the company to rationalize why it operates within a "box" at all.

A sample of how the grid is presented is illustrated on the next page.

PRODUCT/MARKET MATRIX FORMAT

Quadrant One - Present Offerings To Present Markets

As Of Date _____

Prepared By _____

Products   Markets

                Market 1   Market 2   Market 3

Product A   X   X
Product B   X   X
Product C   X   X

Each "X" represents a product matrix "box" to be analyzed

Analagous matrixes are constructed for each of:

> ► **Quadrant Two - Present Offerings to New Markets**
> ► **Quadrant Three - New Products to Present Markets**
> ► **Quadrant Four - New Products to New Markets**

The grid developed describes fully where and how the company competes in the marketplace, and its intentions as now perceived further to operate in the arena. The intentions may alter as a result of the planning process. In fact, unless intentions are changed there are no other possibilities in terms of product and market extension, as distinct from the way product and market presently are exploited.

> This basic laying out is, of course, only preparatory to the _analyses_ to be made in Section 2 to come.

▶ _For convenience, each position marked on the grid will be referred to as a "box". Ultimately, every box has to be analyzed by the company to assure itself why it is involved in a specific box at all and how better to perform within it. How analysis is to be done to meaningful effect will be delineated for you shortly. The essence of strategic planning, however, is maximizing leverage. No company can do everything in each of its chosen market fields at the same time. Nor would it want to because potentials are unequal. Instead, we seek to identify those "boxes" which have the greatest opportunity for powerful leaps forward. Name now, therefore, the three boxes on the grid, that is, product/market categories, which you believe offer the maximum prospect for high reward to the, e.g.:_

BOXES PROMISING MAXIMUM REWARD

Product	**Market (or Market Segment)**
303 Compressor	_Home Improvement_
	Japan
Automatic Aligner	_Machine Shops_
Co-Agitator	_Textile Dyers_

Initiating The Process

Thirty days before the scheduled first meeting of the planning team, the process begins with distribution by the process leader to each member of the planning team the questionnaire illustrated on the next five pages.

The purpose of the questionnaire is trifold:

1. To stimulate the flow of creative juices in each participant

2. To orient the process leader to the beliefs held in the company as the process begins.

3. To identify for the process leader issues, possibly never before enunciated, without the resolution of which the process cannot go forward.

STRATEGIC PLANNING QUESTIONNAIRE

Due Date _____

Name of Company or Profit Center
_____

Planning Team Member Name
_____

Title
_____

Functional Responsibility
_____
_____

SETTING PLANNING PERSPECTIVE

The first step in the strategic planning process is realistic understanding of present position. The expressions of opinion to be given here, then, are to portray the company's operation as you see it today, not what it should or will be in the future. In completing the form, answers should be concise but complete. If more space is needed to elaborate on any point insert a blank sheet, properly indentified.

1. In what business is the company or business unit? (Caution: The answer may not be as obvious as it seems.)

_____
_____

2. What are the characteristics which presently enhance the effectiveness of the organization? (e.g., responsive distribution system, technical innovation, quality image, pricing leadership, efficient manufacturing facilities.)

_____
_____

3. What are the characteristics which limit the effectiveness of the organization? (e.g., inadequate market data, high distribution costs, insufficient sales coverage, lack of productivity standards, structural deficiencies.)

_____

_____

4. Speak not from your own or perceptions within the company, but from the viewpoint of present and prospective customers: <u>what, relative to the competition, is substantially *unique* about the company</u>? (Caution: there are a large number of companies who are *not* substantially unique and participants would be hard pressed to make any entry. Do not confuse *unique* with Item 2. above: characteristics which indeed enhance the effectiveness of the organization but cannot be considered unique. Polaroid, for instance, was unique only until its instant film patent ran out. Essentially the company disintegrated after that. Pfizer has been unique in one product area with its Viagra patent, which apparently is going to hold its strong position until 2020, but, of course, competing products have come along which must be dealt with.

_____

_____

5. What are the most serious competitive threats facing the company? (Is it secure in it's perception of competitor sales, market share?)

_____

_____

_____

_____

6. Who is the best marketer in the company's business universe? If it is not your company, how can your company surpass the capabilities that make that competitor such?

_____

_____

7. What issues, other than those explicitly or implicitly contained in the preceding answers, must be resolved before an effective strategic plan can be generated?

_____

_____

_____

_____

The answers summarize fully where and how the company competes in the marketplace, and its intentions as now perceived further to operate in the arena. The intentions may alter as a result of the planning process. In fact, unless intentions are changed there are no other possibilities in terms of product and market extension, as distinct from the way product and market presently are exploited.

▶ *For convenience, each position marked on the grid will be referred to as a "box". Ultimately, every box has to be analyzed by the company to assure itself why it is involved in a specific box at all and how better to perform within it. How analysis is to be done to meaningful effect will be delineated for you shortly. The essence of strategic planning, however, is maximizing leverage. No company can do everything in each of its chosen market fields at the same time. Nor would it want to because potentials are unequal. Instead, we seek to identify those "boxes" which have the greatest opportunity for powerful leaps forward. Name now, therefore, the <u>three</u> boxes on the grid, that is, product/market categories, which you believe offer the maximum prospect for high reward to the, e.g.:*

BOXES PROMISING MAXIMUM REWARD

Product	**Market (or Market Segment)**
303 Compressor	*Home Improvement*
	Japan
Automatic Aligner	*Machine Shops*
Co-Agitator	*Textile Dyers*

8. What factors have influenced company growth (or decline) and profits (or losses) over the past three years?

_____

_____

_____

_____

9. What do you see as the company's major opportunities for greater achievement? (e.g., new product lines, extending geographical coverage, upgrading quality, production cost reduction)

_____

_____

_____

_____

10. What are the major obstacles to achievement? (e.g., entrenched competition, product obsolescence, labor shortages, declining markets, insufficient resources for plant modernization).

_____

_____

_____

_____

11. What are the most important *strategic* issues you believe must be resolved in seeking a higher level of achievement? (e.g., markets to be served, rate of growth, product scope, degree of risk)

_____

_____

_____

_____

12. Presume everything is possible. If then only _you_ had to make the decision, what should be the three specific and measurable goals for accomplishment through the three-year plan period (e.g., 2014 to 2016). State the goals as results, e.g.:

Goal One:

Double overall revenue from $25 Million to $50 million at EBT of 12%

Goal Two:

Capture 15% of Lilyprod market in Australia

Goal Three:

Reduce rejection rate at Millwood plant from 4% to 1%

The completed questionnaires are submitted to the process leader **_on time_**. The due date is selected to allow the leader enough time to digest the material for both general orientation and identification of "hot issues" to be confronted during the process.

Planning Room Requirements

While much of the effort required over the approximate 60 days it takes to complete the strategic planning process is pursued on company premises, it is important that the key opening and closing planning sessions (two to three days for the first, and one to two days for the second) be held OFF-SITE, for three reasons:

1. The concentration on the process has to be undiluted. Nothing can be more important than plotting the future of the organization nor can any lessened sense of the seriousness of the purpose, easier to occur in the comfort of familiar surroundings, be tolerated.

2. Despite sworn intentions and solemn promises of chief executives, experience has demonstrated that the temptation of participants to leave the meeting room for phone calls, or yield to interruptions by well-meaning fellow employees not on the team, cannot be resisted. Regular break periods are built into the process schedule sufficiently to accommodate whatever communication back to the office may indeed be necessary.

3. It is gross discourtesy for a participant to absent him or herself when another participant is contributing, and calls into question the commitment of the individual.

The sessions site can be a hotel meeting room down the road, or a distant off-site where focus is even more strongly accented, provided it is not seen as opportunity for a lark. Following the decision on where, the mechanical requirements, for the opening and closing off-site sessions, are as follows:

1. A meeting room arranged preferably with tables set up in one to three rows where planning-team participants can sit facing a front work area of at least ten feet in depth. The room should have sufficient wall space for posting many flip-chart sheets, and be comfortable enough in size that participants are not crowded.

2. Four flip-chart pads on easels, procurable at office supply houses. Recommended is 3M EASEL-SIZE POST-IT whose sheets are self-adhering for easy posting. Chart pads of this or other kinds are also usually available at hotels and conference centers, but sometimes at premium prices. Make sure steady-footed easels, with firm backing for the charts, are provided. If other than the 3M brand flip-chart pads are utilized, two rolls of good-grade, 2" wide masking tape are a must.

3. For the process leader, non-bleeding marker pens: 8 each of black, red, green, and blue.

4. A three-ring binder for each participant, for accumulation of worksheet s during the first session and later on into the process. A two-inch spine size is preferable.

Participants should, of course, have pad and pen at hand.

5. The content of certain material accumulated on the flip-chart sheets during days one and two of the first session is recorded by a traffic cop as directed by the leader (see next page re the traffic cop). The process leader will identify which items are so to be recorded. At the send of the first and second days of two or three day session copies of these notes, three-hole punched, are to be available by 10:00 AM of each following morning for distribution to team member. A company secretary may be used for recording and publication if sessions are close to home; at more distant sites a secretarial service can be employed. Alternately, transcribing on a lap-top by one of the participants has proved satisfactory, or even recording by readable hand, so long as duplication capability is available.

6. Always on display in the planning room are a flip-chart sheet, or sheets, on which are posted "to do" tasks accumulated in the process.

Doing It!

The team is now ready to attack actual planning. The basic logic is easily discernible: the team will determine where the company is, where it wants to go, and how its going to get there. There could not be more simplicity. But doing it and making the output work is something else again. There is patience needed not to seek short cutting. At the same time this prompt is conditioned by the imperative to put the plan in place within a reasonable time. The world moves, business moves. It does not wait. We **do not plan future actions**, we **prescribe actions to be initiated** *now* **which will have future effect.**

As the process begins, there is in place:

>   a. The planning team membership.

>   b. The process leader.

>   c. The product/market grid.

>   d. The answered questionnaires. Each individual
>   brings to the planning room a copy of the
>   questionnaire he or she has submitted.

The Traffic Cop

A final preliminary to be attended to as the team goes to work is taken care of at the beginning of the first day of the first planning session: the appointment of one of the planning team members to be a "traffic cop" in this way:

In the course of the process, assignments are made not just for the team members in the planning room, but also to individuals not on the team.

There is data to be gathered, information to be disseminated, deadlines to be reminded of, conferences between individuals to be scheduled. Tracking is necessary to insure smooth flow and good control of the process. This is accomplished by appointing a "traffic cop", a team member who is responsible for monitoring fulfillment of elements on time, including, if necessary, following up personally with individuals to assure compliance. Aside from general sharing of the load on the process leader, a specific reason for this adjutant is that the traffic cop often will have to do the note taking as the leader holds forth at the front of the room.

Establishing The Strategic Mind Set

We have said the planning team is formed out of recognition by the chief executive that utilizing all the talents in the organization is the best course to achieving the best result. The corollary to this is that each team member during the course must cast him or herself in the mold of the chief executive and think as a chief executive must. (Indeed, some in the room may already be aspirants to the responsibility and every one in the group should be considered as having at least latent capability to assume the job.)

Strategic planning is a thinking exercise. Creative thinking is the highest form of mental usage. Discipline will be applied to the hard plan that will be the output of the process, but in its course we strive for release of powers to conceive the new, the different, the daring, the radical if need be…to reach for the stars! We are iconoclasts and innovators, inventors and pioneers. If the team is so cast the greatest success will be achieved. Hence, as the activity begins the leader, the chief executive and all of the individuals urge themselves to the state of *the strategic mind* set.

First Day

1. To begin the live process in earnest the leader calls on the principal financial officer to summarize briefly for the team the operating performance of the company over the last three years. Certainly most managers on the team will be familiar with these results, but the iteration is to highlight the perspective on what has been against which the what to be plotted is to be measured.

2. The leader posts on a convenient place on the meeting room wall a sheet marked "TO DO", on which will be recorded tasks and assignments – with dates for completion – determined to be necessary in the course of the deliberations. Sheet are added as appropriate.

3. The leader reminds the group of the four essentials for planning covered in section on Why Strategic Planning Doesn't Work above, i.e., Methodology, Reach, Discipline, The Horses, each of which are integral to plan generation.

4. Because the team members are not bloodless automatons, the leader posts in prominent positions around the room reinforcements to consciousness of what the group is about as it engages the concrete work of planning, in nature such as these:

THE NEW, THE DIFFERENT, THE BETTER...AND IF NOTHING LESS WILL DO... THE *RADICAL*!"

"Would you tell me which way I ought to go from here?" asked Alice.
"That depends a good deal on where you want to get," said the Cat.
"I really don't care where" replied Alice.
"Then it doesn't much matter which way you go," said the Cat.
                                        - Lewis Carroll, Alice's Adventures in Wonderland

THE STRATEGIC PLAN WE'RE DEVELOPING REPRESENTS *WHAT WE'RE GOING TO DO!*

"What business strategy is all about; what distinguishes it from all other kinds of business planning - is, in a word, competitive advantage. Without competitors there would be no need for strategy, for the sole purpose of strategic planning is to enable the company to gain, as effectively as possible, a sustainable edge over its competitors"

- Keniche Ohnae, *The Mind Of The Strategist*

STRATEGIC PLANNING AT ITS HEART IS SIMPLY A RECITATION OF WHERE WE ARE …WHERE WE"RE GOING… AND HOW WE'RE GOING TO GET THERE!

SECTION TWO

Determining Where The Company Stands Now

A. Establishing How Well The Company Meets The Expectations Of Its Stakeholders

The process leader, working from the front of the planning room, elicits from the team members before him the information following. In so doing he or she nurtures participation by each team member and allows neither domination by the articulate nor reticence by the diffident. Whatever is heard is recorded, without judgment, on the flip charts standing in the front of the room. The questions the leader asks are:

1. Who are the stakeholders?

Caution: the leader does *not* work from a list. It is important that team members gain a refined appreciation of just who are the stakeholders — the number of whom will vary from company to company - and the relative importance of each. A typical listing might be a selection from the sort of the following:

Customers*
Owners
Employees
Lenders
Suppliers
Community
Professional Community

---

*Customers *always* are to be listed number one and, it is to be hoped, are the first category voiced by the team members. Customers define a business. Obviously, if a company does not have customers, or potential customers, it does not have a business, and nothing else need be said.

The process leader then guides the group in reduction of the undiscriminated namings of constituents to an agreed-upon list. That is, the constituents deemed to be of critical importance. These he transcribes to a single flip-sheet, discarding the others.

2. For the stakeholders now listed, what precisely does each expect of management?

> Again, the leader gives no hints but should expect to hear expectations like: earnings, growth, responsiveness, career opportunity, quality, technical innovation, TLC, reliability.

The leader similarly guides the reduction of the items called-out to an agreed-upon prime listing of expectations for each stakeholder. These are posted on a single flip-chart sheet for each.

3. At this point, some on the team might be sitting back and thinking, *"This isn't going to b demanding at all."* But the leader now directs:

Evaluate, for each stakeholder now listed, how well you believe the company meets each particular expectation. Do this on a scale of I to IV in which the ratings are:

I = Excellently
II = Pretty well
III = Marginally
IV = We stink!

The leader goes around the room and asks from each team member a rating on each of the expectations posted. He marks alongside each item, in a different color, *only the lowest rating heard*. The reason for this is that progress is best fostered by taking the stringent view.

4. The leader now goes around the room again and asks each team member to evaluate, for each stakeholder expectation, how *important* it is that, *as managers of the company,* we satisfy the expectation. The ratings are on a scale of A to D in which:

> **A = Essential**
> **B = Pretty important**
> **C = Marginally important**
> **D = We couldn't care less**

The leader marks on the item listing, in a third color, *only the highest rating heard*. This is because it would be incomprehensible if managers did not aspire to the highest performance standard sought by stakeholders.

The leader now circles in red those pairs of ratings displayed, of "how well" and "how important" expectations are addressed, which show a discrepancy of more than one level between them. That is:

If a rating pair were shown, say, to be IA or IIIB, they would be on the same level or only one apart.

If, however, the pair were shown to be, say, ID or IVB, a two or three level discrepancy would be described.

THE RESULTANT CIRCLINGS OF DISCREPANCIES INDICATING SIGNIFICANT DIFFERENTIALS SUGGEST THE EXISTENCE OF **ISSUES** WHICH MAY HAVE TO BE RESOLVED BEFORE A STRATEGIC PLAN CAN BE PUT IN PLACE.

This identification, of ISSUES to be resolved is the whole business of the early part of the process. At this stage it is unknown if any particular item is validly an issue or important enough to be contended with. That deciding will be made in due course, but the raw starting points must be established.

WE ARE NOT, THEN, INTERESTED IN THE *LISTINGS* WE CONSTRUCT IN THEMSELVES, BUT IN THE **ISSUES** THEY UNCOVER. WE ARE SEEKING TO DISCERN THOSE ISSUES WHICH *MUST* BE RESOLVED WITHIN THE PLAN'S PLOT OR ITS EFFICACY WOULD BE COMPROMISED.

5. Each of the marked-up consensus sheets are now posted on the walls of the meeting room, to remain clearly visible as the session continues. The rule is that once any item is posted it must be considered as an established guide point and cannot be contradicted unless the group concludes the item itself has to be revisited. The content of these sheets, or the notes of the traffic cop recording them, are the ones to be duplicated, sheet for sheet, for distribution the next morning, and inclusion in each participant's binder for continued ready reference as the process proceeds both during the sessions and in the approximate 60-day period before the strategic plan is put in final form.

B. What Is Unique About The Company?

The Comparative Breakout Technique

A key technique frequently to be used by the process leader during the course of the process is to break up the full planning team into smaller groups which go off to any convenient place on the premises – an empty conference room or office, a lobby corner perhaps, or even poolside - to pursue defined assignments to be completed within a defined time period.

For a planning team of, say, nine to twelve participants, the breakups would be into three or four groups of three each. For a planning team of six, three groups of two would serve well. (For a full team as small as three members, or even two, the subdivisions would be single individuals.) The make-up of the smaller groups is rotated for each breakout session, for maximum cross-pollination and to obviate laziness fostered by comfort.

When time is up the teams return and post the results of their deliberations on the flip-chart sheets at the front of the planning room. The process leader than leads the forum in comparison and evaluation of the several outputs and reduction of these to a single output on which the planning team as a whole, and the chief executive as affirmer, puts its imprimatur.

This comparative approach to hardening input will be utilized a number of times as the process proceeds.

The technique normally is first employed in the process at this point.

♦BREAKOUT SESSION: Time allotment:
30 minutes

Identify What Characteristic(s) Make The Company Substantially Unique

The assignment for each breakout group is to define what, in respect to its competitors on the playing field on which it competes, is substantially unique about the company **and has meaning to customers**. Participants have already been asked this in Question 4 on the Strategic Planning Questionnaire distributed prior to the first planning session. The same answers can be put on the table for evaluation. The mini group comes to a consensus on its determination. IT IS NOT AT ALL UNCOMMON FOR A TEAM TO COME UP EMPTY! To enunciate more than one uniqueness would be rare. Often, relative advantages can be identified but true uniqueness is hard to come by. Relative advantages may be the characteristics determined in the answer to Question 2 on the Strategic Planning Questionnaire, that is, strengths which enhance the effectiveness of the organization.

When the breakout groups return to the planning room each posts the results of its deliberations on the flip charts. The expectation would be that each of the placements would be identical, including the possibility that nothing at all could be entered. If, in fact, there are entries which are not identical the process leader guides the discussion to reducing the opinions to a single list. Either way, only the consensus arrived at is left posted on a wall.

Whatever is concluded, an ISSUE may have been identified. If no uniqueness has been identified, how is the company is to achieve such? Or, how further can it exploit the uniqueness it does possess?

The traffic cop replicates and distributes the copies of postings for inclusion in the participants' strategic planning binders.

C. What Obstacles Stand In The Way Of The Company?

♦ **BREAKOUT SESSION: Time allotment:**
                    1 hour (typically)

Identify The Problems and Deficiencies That Are Impediments To The Company's Prosperity

The process leader reshuffles the breakout teams, again to avoid the comfort of sitting with the same individuals though all the iterations. Their object now is to list all *significant* difficulties the company faces in maximizing performance and growth. These can be both internal and external factors. Again, these are the same characteristics and factors which limit the effectiveness of the organization asked for in Questions 3 and 10 of the Strategic Planning Questionnaire (Examples given in Question 3 were: inadequate market data, high distribution costs, insufficient sales coverage, lack of productivity standards, structural deficiencies, entrenched competition, product obsolescence, labor shortages, declining markets, insufficient resources for plant modernization). The range over which any individual company might identify impediments is very wide.

The listings the breakout teams develop might in the first pass be quite long even when the limitation to *significant* is imposed. The job now is to judge which, if no other efforts were to be mounted, are deemed to be the top three or four necessary to be overcome most beneficially to allow the company to seek its destiny. The leader will remind the teams not to neglect consideration of factors of political climate, economic conditions, social imperatives and technological development to which specific responses may have to be made. Each group culls its entries and comes up with its definitive conclusions.

The breakout teams return to the planning room and each posts its single, refined list. The leader now once more guides reduction of the separate lists to a single list, and then elicits from the whole planning team which of the surviving entries are identified as ISSUES.

D. What Are The Company's Opportunities?

♦**BREAKOUT SESSION: Time allotment:**
                    1 hour (typically)

Identify The Specific Areas of Opportunity Available

The process leader again shuffles the breakout teams. The charge to each team now is to list all *significant*, real-world opportunities the company at this point thinks are pursuable. Once more these have already been compiled preliminarily in the answers in the Strategic Planning Questionnaire to Question 9.

To start, each breakout team member repeats his or her original answers on the questionnaire. If, as the rhythm and flavor of the process takes hold, CREATIVITY has have been spurred enough, newly occurring ideas are likely and welcomed. There is no limit to the items proposed by either the individuals or the breakout team *in toto*.

The team reduces the propositions accumulated to the top three or four it believes have the highest potential for magnitude company progress. One reason for the parings that will constantly be applied during the process in that no company could attack simultaneously all it might conceive. Its purposes can best and only be served by an understanding of where action will enable the greatest leverage.

The groups return to the planning room and institute the comparison and reduction protocol with which they are now familiar. The result is posted on the wall and noted for planning binder inclusion by the traffic cop.

Each now of the three or four major opportunities displayed likely can be interpreted as ISSUES to be attacked.

E. Analyzing The Product/Market Matrix "Boxes"

♦ **BREAKOUT SESSION: Time allotment:**
                        1 to 2 hours (typically)

Choose The "Boxes" To Be Subjected To Rigorous Analysis, By Whom? And How?

The breakout teams memberships are shuffled once again and dispatched.

The teams, or individuals in some cases, refer to the three choices made as the last item in answer to question 7 in the planning questionnaire, i.e., those product/market boxes believed to offer the maximum prospect for reward to the company and that, therefore, must be subjected to critical examination.

N.B. If an existing mainstay product/market box has not been selected for analysis, out of perception that market position is firmly established and its future astutely-directed, wisdom still suggests analysis anyway.

Other "boxes" (limited in number) which seem to hold promise, if not quite at the level evaluated for the top three candidates, may also be added. Indeed over the course of the first plan year, every "box" on the complete product/market matrix array must be rationalized to assure tight business discipline.

The dispersed teams again engage in winnowing choices offered by the individual members to those three assessed to be the top highest potential candidates for company opportunity. Again, the number of "three" highest potential boxes is not to be considered an absolute limit.

The last determination the teams make is *who*, individually or in concert with others, is to make each analysis. The individual almost always is a member of the full planning team; *others assigned may or may not be planning team members* but are considered appropriately equipped to carry out the assignment.

The teams return to the planning room. The leader again initiates a comparison and reduction-to-adopted-choices protocol. The results are posted on the wall and copied by the traffic cop for reproduction, distribution and inclusion in each participant's planning binder.

The chosen "boxes" identified can in themselves be considered ISSUES.

> The analysis of the "boxes" rarely can be completed in the planning room because it is unlikely that all the information required is at hand - *it may not yet exist anywhere in the company* - nor could assessments adequate enough for the company to bet its money on be definitively made.

Instead, the leader guides the team in <u>modeling</u> how the scrutiny of a "box" is to be pursued. Two of the boxes on the sheets posted are selected for the exercise by consensus of the full team. **Real world examples in the company's real business universe are used for illustration**. The workup is pursued so:

♦   **MODEL PRODUCT/MARKET MATRIX   "BOX" ANALYSIS**

> For every business, from corner bakery to industrial giant, all consideration begins and ends with the customer. Analysis has meaning only in relation to the satisfaction of the customer.

The universe of every enterprise, of course, is the customer body, the company, and *the competition*. Competitors must be evaluated as rigorously as the company. Especially to be avoided is the trap of ignorance of what makes competitors tick.

The task of the leader in the modeling exercise is to elicit and moderate the judgments offered by the full team assembled on each element under examination. The assessments cannot be considered definitive in this first pass, but are made to imbue each team member with understanding how to proceed in the intersession period which will follow this initial planning session.

A prime step is to determine what are the wants of customers across the full range of their requirements? When these are listed on the flipchart sheets the leader asks the team members to call out their ratings, on a scale of I to 10, where 10 is the highest, of how well the company and its competitors meet the customers' expectations. Just as in rating earlier how well the company meets expectation of its stakeholders, the leader accepts the *worst* rating put forward for the company, but the *best* heard for the competitor. (It is common for company personnel to downgrade the competition: "They're price cutters" or "They make payoffs" or "Their product is crap." Likely the comments are less grounded in fact than in expression of loyalty to the company; it may be that the same kind of accusations are made against the company. Clearly, competitors must be assured objectively or how to get the edge on them is much more difficult to surmise.

▶Note that in the example analysis form next laid out a single column is assigned to competitors. Only rarely, of course, would there be a single competitor. More often there are several principal competitors so that in the definitive analysis there must be separate columns for Competitor A, Competitor B, Competitor C and so on. In situations where a company has numerous competitors, just a few of the most representative are appropriately examined.

PRODUCT/MARKET ANALYSIS EXAMPLE

A. Product

Name   FuguTron 444

Market   U.S. Bowling Alleys

Market Size: $(000) _____

Company Market Share :   ____ %

Competition Market Share: ____%

Competitor A   ____ %
Competitor B   ____ %
Competitor C   ____ %

                       etc.

B. How Market Players Satisfy Customers

(On a scale of 0 to 10)

	How The Company Satisfies Wants	How Competition Satisfies Wants*
Want A	9	8
Want B	7	8
Want C	0	5
		etc.

*estimates may be made collectively or by individual competitors as most appropriate

C. The Market Scenario

A narrative exposition of what will happen in the market place for the particular product category, independent of what the company might do.

The elements to be contained, in more detail than within the Questionnaire answers, are:

- total market size
- company market share
- competitor market shares
- estimated growth rate
- the authority for these values
- changes anticipated from technological advances
- other market influences, like regulatory requirements, societal changes

D. How Players Differentiate Themselves Now

	The Company	**The Competition***
Marketing Thrust		
Product Features		
Service		
Other (specify)		

collectively or by individual competitors as appropriate

E.   How Further The Company Could Differentiate Itself

Inspect the answers to how presently the company differentiates itself in the market place as reported in D. above. Stretch conception now to how the company could gain further advantage by innovative action of any kind in altering the original answers. Enumerate specifically:

<u>Company Opportunities For Further Differentation</u>

- *Change In Marketing Thrust*

- *Improved Product*

- *Product Acquisition*

- *Improved Service*

- *Other (specify)*

THIS, HOW THE COMPANY CAN FURTHER DIFFERENTIATE ITSELF, IS THE HEART OF STRATEGY

The whole of strategy development is directed to gaining advantage over the competition. If there were no competition there is no need for strategy; just run a nice neat shop and send out the invoices. The leader begins by asking the team to determine what are the wants of customers across the full range of their requirements. When these are listed on the flipchart sheets the leader asks the team members to call out their ratings, on a scale of I to 10 where 10 is the highest, of how well the company and its competitors meet the customers' expectations. Just as in rating earlier how well the company meets expectation of its stakeholders, the leader accepts the *worst* rating put forward for the company, <u>but</u> the *best* heard for the competitor. (It is common for company personnel to downgrade the competition. "They're price cutters" or "They make payoffs" or "Their product is crap." Likely the comments are not grounded in fact or may be only expressions of loyalty to the ship, and it may be that the same kind of accusations are made against the team's company. Clearly, competitors must be measured objectively or how to get the edge on them is much more difficult to surmise.

Upon completion of the model analysis exercise, a second candidate, preferably one much different in terms both of product and market, is subjected to the same treatment. The intent is to indoctrinate team members in the way the analyses are is to be done and understood before the actual definitive analyses are made during the planning process intersession to come.

F. Designate The Product/Market Matrix "Boxes" Rigorously To Be Analyzed By Whom

♦ **BREAKOUT SESSION: Time allotment:**
                    1 to 2 hours

The Definitive Analyses

Modeling a product/market "box" in the planning room is one thing, but to establish the *definitive* analyses on which decisions will be based is quite another. Research and information-gathering may be required in varying degree. Opinions have to replaced with fact, or if factual information is not available (competitors, e.g., are unlikely to reveal to you their market shares) by considered judgments whose basis can be justified. Ratings which were tossed out off the tops of heads up to this point now have to reflect the considered appraisal on particular points of the most knowledgeable people in the company. Reasonable time, of course, is required to obtain information not already available within the company and to complete the variety of tasks entailed.

The definitive analyses, then, are made in the **INTERSESSION** period which occurs between the first and second plenary planning sessions The process leader now undertakes confirmation of *just which* of the "boxes" designated by the breakout teams as promising the most bang for the buck indeed are to be analyzed. The concurrence of the chief executive in the choices is an obvious necessity.

The breakout teams have already, under the "By Whom" charge under Section E, selected the individuals, *within or without the planning teams,* deemed most competent for the task. The process leader elicits confirmation of the appointments from the floor and, as appropriate, will ask the chief executive for his or her agreement with these.

The analyses are to be strictly market-based. Companies live and die in the bazaar, not in the boardroom or functional haven. This might suggest that the scrutinies have to be done by sales and marketing personnel. If that were the case too much burden might be based on one or a few individuals. But beyond that, each team member, by the very nature of the process, assumes the role of chief executive. If the individuals are true managers each of them should have enough knowledge of the company, and smarts, to be capable of doing a "box", drawing on others, as appropriate, for data and information. A benefit to this construct is that it affords the chief executive an excellent vehicle for estimation of individual abilities

A time frame is established for the completion of each "box" analysis. The schedule is posted on the "to do" list always on display in the planning room, and recorded by the traffic cop for distribution to each team member.

N.B.: The analyses, oddly, are absolutely essential to plan to plan formulation but are destined to become support and reference material, not elements to be themselves in the plan proper. Their purpose is to be a principal insurer of plan integrity.

As true planning progresses no course chosen can contradict the content of any "box". There could not, for instance, be within the plan a target of achieving a certain dollar sales volume if such volume were beyond what a box has decreed as the total volume available in the market. If at that point the proponent of the variant number can give evidence that the box number was wrong, a question is to be raised as to why the "box" was not done properly and why the proponent did not bring up the matter previously. Such situations are to be eschewed. The care given to reliable, final "boxes" cannot be compromised.

G. Confirm The Company's *Present* Strategic Intent

There is always existent in every company a strategic intent. It may be well and explicitly expressed and clearly understood by every one in the company. Or it may be vague, fuzzy and hardly discernible to more than a few. What strategic intent *will be* as a result of the planning process may be the same, similar or radically different. In any case statement of the present intent is necessary to complete the Phase One task of establishing where the company is as it begins.

The chief executive should be able to state the company's present intent and no more need to be said. But can the chief do so? Maybe. Maybe not. And if the individual can enunciate intent, does everyone in the organization understand it? Does everyone perceive how it is to be implemented? At the very least a cross check likely is in order.

Before anything else can be attempted the company has to confirm what its fundamental driving force has been in the past and decide what the choice is to be for the future. For some companies identification of what the force has been is easy to arrive at; for others it is less clear whether the company, in contrast to belief, has in fact been driven by market, by product, by technology, by sales method.

Validate Company's Current Strategic Intent

The leader dispatches the latest reshuffled breakout teams. Their assignment is dual.

1. To return with a simple statement of the company's current strategic intent. *Not* what it *should be*, but what it *is*.

> E.g.,   "Be the low cost producer",
>   "Dominate the high end market"
>   "Establish quality leadership".

2. Rate on a scale of 1 up to 10, how well the company is implementing the strategy.

Seldom should there be debate on the first item, unless the company is in such serious disarray that no strategy at all is recognizable. The rating in the second item may prove to be useful in getting at what kind of metamorphosis the company may have to undertake.

The subgroups return to the planning room and post their results. The leader directs comparison and reduction to a single two-item sheet, once again for continuing display on the room wall and inclusion in the planning binders.

SUMMARY OF SECTION TWO ACTIVITY

The purpose of the effort in Section Two was to establish WHERE THE COMPANY IS as it undertakes the planning process. On the walls around them the team is surrounded by the results of the effort so far. No strategic planning has been done, except that hints of it may lie in the model product/market analyses produced. The leader reminds that all of the posted sheets will be replicated for distribution and retention in the planning binders, to which reference will be made whenever necessary to insure the integrity of the process as it proceeds.

The leader recites briefly, and asks for confirmation from the floor that the team has:

1. Assessed how well the company meets the expectations of its stakeholders.

2. Established whether or not the company possesses uniqueness.

3. Identified the major impediments to its progress.

4. Identified the principal opportunities it so far believes are available to the company.

5. Has laid out for analysis the most promising "boxes" on its product/market matrix.

6. Has affirmed present strategic intent.

At the same time, the leader notes that issues to be confronted within these elements have been marked.

The grand question is then put to the team:

Presuming the product/market analyses will reliably be completed, does what we have done fairly and accurately state the position of the company as it initiates strategic planning?

Caution: the leader does not accept easy assent but emphasizes that, unless a solid platform has been established, faultiness in the plotting to come is a hazard. The leader says, in effect: "Speak now, or forever hold your peace." If anyone does speak, the objection or demurrer has to be resolved before the team can move on.

For edification, here is a well-done statement of position formulated by one company:

"(xxxx) is the *de facto* outsourcing partner for creating massive Internet and on-line digital content. We build trust from our client-partners by adding value to their initiatives, communicating proactively and decisively, and making written commitments which we reliably meet. We build loyalty from our investors by delivering significant shareholder value, which we achieve by setting - and consistently meeting - our goals.

As (xxxx) enters 2001 it takes pride in the accomplishments achieved through 2000 and looks further to exploiting the position it has established as the premier provider of digital content outsourcing. From a revenue volume of $ _____ in 1999, a level of $_____ was attained in 2000, while earnings grew from $_____ to $_____. We look forward now to reaching a volume level in 2002 of $____ at earnings of $___.

A key element in assuring continuation on this success track is our embrace of XML technology, reflected most directly in establishing our XML Content Factory in (xxxx). We will continue to focus on strategic partnerships with clients with whom we work on a highly consultative basis. In our prospect universe are a near-infinite number of textual, audio and video data sources which need to be made available on the Web. A significant number of these will provide this data variety in XML form. The "heavy lifting" of transforming data is the forte of (xxxx), supporting its intention to become the outsourcer of choice.

(xxxx) will expand its toolset to create effective barriers to entry by others, and to optimize through technology our efficiencies. In creating natural extensions to our core capabilities we expect to be integrating audio and video digital data to enable high-value content for our clients. In the latter part of 2001 we will begin seeking acquisitions to expand our own efforts in integrating new capabilities. We expect at the same time to be growing our consulting and professional services business and will build on our European Services Center to exploit the potential of that area. Still further to strengthen our market position we will be creating vendor partnerships.

We are cognizant of the challenges of building organization and management abilities sufficient to perform with distinction through a period of continuing expansion. Substantial address to this is included in our strategic plan. Coupled with our accent on innovation we are confident of our ability to maintain a high rate of growth and profitability."

> **In other words this company had an acute sense of itself and what it wanted to be!**

SECTION THREE

Establishing The Company's Ambitions

A. The Vision Expression

The planning team is now almost ready to begin plotting the company's course. But what course? *Does the organization, first of all, have a vision, not of what it is, but what it wants itself to be?*

A company pursuing the strategic planning process may already have in place a vision expression, or mission statement, or some similarly named attempt to define its aspirations. The existing expression may be entirely adequate as it stands and needs only to be confirmed, or it may be that slight revision would be useful, or it might be apparent that a gross restatement is necessary to respond to a set of conditions much changed from the time of the statement's origination

The vision expression, although it is often included in annual reports for public consumption, *is primarily for the orientation of every employee on the payroll, and all future employees to come.* It instructs just what the company is striving to be come whether or not is yet at the level it seeks. Once established, all action in the company is directed to carrying out the ambition embraced. Hence it is the overall ruler of strategic planning.

► Basic to establishing the vision expression, the company has to confirm what its fundamental driving force has been in the past and affirm what the choice is to be for the future. For some companies identification of what the force has been is easy to arrive at; for others it is less clear whether the company, in contrast to belief, has in fact been driven by market, by product, by technology, by sales method, or something else.

What should the expression be?

The answer is: WHATEVER YOU WANT IT TO BE!, so long as it unequivocally communicates the expectations the company imposes on itself. The expression has to be concise and easily understood.

Many avowals are constructed in a manner like this:

> *(x) is the de facto outsourcing partner for creating massive Internet and on-line digital content. We build trust from our client-partners by adding value to their initiatives, communicating proactively and decisively, and making written commitments which we reliably meet. We build loyalty from our investors by delivering significant shareholder value, which we achieve by setting - and consistently meeting - our goals.*

On the other hand, a famous software company, whose products you use everyday, once adopted an aegis that read simply:

> *"A computer on every desk and in every home"*

Microsoft did not even make computers, except in its very earliest days, but recognized that by facilitating their usefulness the demand for its software products would constantly expand.

The point is, the vision expression becomes a mantra emblazoned on the forehead of everyone in the company, focusing where effort is constantly to be directed and barring activities that do not support the intent. For this reason, lengthy vision expressions are discouraged because they cannot be remembered and are therefore poor guides to day-to-day sense of purpose.

Vision expressions are expected to remain valid for a long time but not necessarily permanently as the business landscape changes. For example,

Microsoft's vision later was contained in a less succinct affirmation of: "*Connected PC and connected TV.*" We were to understand from this the idea of integrating the intelligence and interactivity of PCs with the video and sound of TV "to enable people and businesses throughout the world to realize their full potential" [including video games?]. But some might argue the new expression was a diminishment in acuity. The company now publishes a flowery (and grammatically defective) encompassing of aspiration whose superiority to earlier attempts also is unclear.

Over the years the author has concluded that, whatever form of vision expression might suit public relations and employee handbook purposes, companies who want to make their strategic planning declarations vibrantly active are best served by the shortest possible statement that conveys the essence of aspirations.

CAUTION: To be rejected forthwith are elements included in the vision expression as window dressing with little serious intent to act in accordance with them. If, for instance, a company were to assert its concern for the community but does nothing to demonstrate it, it will be seen as untrustworthy and all of its statements dubious. One of the worst offenses occurs when a company expresses a high level of commitment to the benefit of its employees and then is scorned by these from the insincerity apparent in the way it acts.

Examples of the variety of approaches companies have adopted follow. As you peruse these, glean what may be useful in developing *your* company's vision expression, but the end aim is to make *your* expression distinctive and an accurate portrayal of what *you* want *your* company to be perceived as.

a. **Concise, nicely specific, yet wide ranging in its embrace:**

"*At IBM we strive to lead in the creation, development and manufacture of the industry's most advanced information technologies, including computer systems, software, networking systems, storage devices and microelectronics.*

We translate these advanced technologies into value for our customers through our professional solutions and services businesses worldwide."

b. **Short, but what exactly the organization does is not clear:**

"The American Cancer Society is the nationwide community-based voluntary health organization dedicated to eliminating cancer as a major health problem by preventing cancer, saving lives, and diminishing suffering from cancer, through research, education, advocacy, and service."

c. **Brief, pithy:**

"Studio 67 is to be a great place to eat, combining an intriguing atmosphere with excellent, interesting food that is also very good for the people who eat there. We want fair profit for the owners, and a rewarding place to work for the employees."

d. **Short, indecipherable to outsiders, but exquisitely appropriate for the particular company at the point in time it was adopted:**

"MS/MS at MS prices"

e. **Short, platitudinous, doesn't tell what business the company is in:**

"Our Goal: To be an enduring, respected, and profitable company. Our partnerships will prosper by creating an environment in which our customers and team members/owners will be better off tomorrow than they are today."

f. **Short, sweet, and smartly ambitious:**

"People love our clothes and trust our company.

We will market the most appealing and widely worn casual clothing in the world

We will clothe the world."

(Levi Strauss)

g. **Workmanlike, but rather clumsy:**

"Electric Editors aims to become the primary source on the Internet for everyone looking to satisfy a professional need related to the publication of the written word, and the primary medium of communication between in-house and freelance staff. It is a joint venture set up by a group of editors seeking to harness the Internet as an effective medium and resource for professionals across the whole spectrum of publishing activity."

h. Much too ponderous to be a mantra. Better to have sharpened the first two sentences, stopped, and used the balance of the material elsewhere:

"<u>STATEMENT OF PURPOSE</u>

Bruker AXS stands for high-technology and high quality standards. We develop and manufacture sophisticated analytical X-ray systems for applications in life science, lab and process automation, and material analysis.

- *We define technological trends*
- *We offer turnkey solutions*

PARTNERSHIP WITH CUSTOMERS

- *Our solutions are based on the needs of our customers*
- *Global presence ensures competent local support*
- *Reliability and continuity is the basis for a long-term relationship*

TEAM WORK

- *Cooperation of all employees is the basis of our success*
- *We operate based on objectives developed out of our self-understanding our visions and our strategies*
- *Our leadership and attitude goals give us direction and determine the rules for the team work*

- *Every employee understands his/her role in the organization*
- *A sense of ownership drives his/her thinking and actions*
- *His/her personality is characterized by the willingness to learn and adapt to changing needs*

ECONOMIC SUCCESS ENSURES THE FUTURE
OF THE BUSINESS

- *We are striving for healthy profitability to allow investment in future innovation and business growth, and to satisfy shareholder requirements"*

i. Grandiose, and dubious:

"Corporate Vision: Our vision is 'people making history by making a difference.' It is built on creating a multi-regional leadership position on a physically balanced platform that will produce sustainable above-industry average earnings growth. We believe that our model combined with our strategic location and highly-incentivized employees will allow our company to realize that vision and become one the top investment choices in our industry over the long term.

Corporate Mission: Our mission is to transform the lives of millions of people by providing reliable, reasonably priced energy and related services in an environmentally responsible manner. We're working to make our vision a reality by successfully completing our mission in a manner that serves all of our stakeholders, including: shareholders, customers, employees, communities and the environment."

(Cinergy, a utility company)

j. The first sentence of the following effort about does it, after which the enthusiasm of the formulators carried them into details belonging elsewhere.

"OptIPuter's mission is to enable collaborating scientists to interactively explore massive amounts of previously uncorrelated data by developing a radical new architecture for a number of this decade's e-Science shared information technology facilities. Observing that the exponential growth rates in bandwidth and storage are now much higher than Moore's Law, this research exploits a new world in which the central architectural element is optical networking, not computers. This transition is caused by the use of parallelism, as in supercomputing a decade ago. However, this time the parallelism is in multiple wavelengths of light, or lambdas, on single optical fibers, creating "supernetworks."

The OptIPuter project aims at the re-optimization of the entire grid stack of software abstractions, learning how to "waste" bandwidth and storage in order to conserve "scarce" computing in this new world of inverted values. Essentially, the OptIPuter is a "virtual" parallel computer in which the individual "processors" are widely distributed clusters; the "memory" is in the form of large distributed data repositories; "peripherals" are very-large scientific instruments, visualization displays and/or sensor arrays; and the "motherboard" uses standard IP delivered over multiple dedicated lambdas. The southern California-based and Chicago-based research teams are prototyping the OptIPuter initially on campus, metropolitan and state-wide optical fiber networks. Beyond servicing the scientific and engineering research communities, the OptIPuter can be an enabling technology for broader societal needs, including emergency response, homeland security, health services, and science education."

k. Too general, and the loftiness is hoped to be genuine, but GE, of course, is in many disparate businesses, so that it is the vision expressions of its component divisions that have to be looked to for authentic vision statements:

"GE recognizes that part of being a successful and well-respected company is being socially responsible. GE is committed to serve the communities where we do business, to provide our customers with innovative, high-quality products and services and to protect the health of our workers and our environment."

How to establish *your* company's vision expression:

♦ BREAKOUT SESSION: Time allotment:
45 minutes

Planning sub-teams are formed and depart for their enclaves away from the planning room.

The charge to them is:

a. If a vision expression already exists, confirm that it fully satisfies.

b. If it exists but is not satisfactory, rewrite it.

c. If none exists, create one.

When the sub-teams return to the planning room they record on flip chart sheets the vision expression each has constructed. If there were three groups dispatched, say, three vision statements would appear before the full team.

The leader directs comparison of the separate offerings. Perhaps all are similar, perhaps all are different, and gradations among them may be slight or major. The result is reduction to a single statement, once again posted for display on the planning room wall throughout the duration of the planning sessions, and recorded by the traffic cop for replication and inclusion in the participants planning binders.

The vision statement to this point is a *tentative* expression, to be validated as the process proceeds.

B. What Is A Goal?

Presumably the organization had some idea of where it wants to go before the planning effort started. (But not necessarily!) Usually, the chief executive and others enter the planning room with at least a general conception of what they would like to see happen to the company. Whether they do or do not, the ambitions cannot be generalities: like, "Be the product innovator", "Grow rapidly", "Make a lot of money". Such are akin to being in favor of motherhood and apple pie, laudable but not useful.

Rather, company ambitions have to be expressed as hard goals or they cannot become anything likely to be realized, - or assessable if they were.

Goals *must* be:

SPECIFIC - directed to a concrete aspect of the business.

MEASURABLE - a visible number, percentage, dimension.

ATTAINABLE - not beyond the resources available to, or procurable by, the company, nor the dimensions of the market itself.

RATIONAL – represent a reach but do not test reason.

TIME BASED - to be attained within a defined period of time.

C. Setting The Goals

Only a limited number of overall goals can be essayed by a company. Three or four is the limit; just one or two could be fully acceptable. Any company which tries to make a wish-list a set of goals is doomed probably to achieving none of them.

Goals are set for a three year plan period corresponding to calendar or fiscal years. A longer period would go too far beyond that for which reasonable projections could be made. Shorter periods would not allow sufficient time for significant strategic actions to be proven effective.

♦BREAKOUT SESSION: Time allotment:
1 hour

Breakout teams are reshuffled and dispersed. The assignment to each now is to propose the single overall goal of the company, plus not less than one, nor more than three other goals, which in fact are significant elements within the overall goal.

The starting point for the subgroup deliberations are each individual's answers to question 12 of the Strategic Planning Questionnaire where it was asked, *"If then only you had to make the decision, what should be the three specific and measurable goals for accomplishment through the three-year period, 200_ to -200_? State the goals as results."*

> ▶ How a goal is easily identified lies in that last word. If a <u>result</u> is expressed by the goal stated it is a proper goal; otherwise it is <u>not</u>.

The overall goal for a business is *always* the sales or revenue volume, at a desired operating profit, to be achieved by the company in the third year of the plan. (Not-for-profit organizations must do strategic planning too, but would not express their principal goal this way, yet still must obey the process rules.). All businesses in a free market economy can have no other overall goal than financial prosperity.

The subsidiary goals which are also set in place will be seen simply as major components of the overall goal. These component goals may touch upon any area of company activity which has strong impact on the prime goal. They might cover such items as specific market penetrations, enhanced distribution, new product introductions, new factory facilities, quality performance. Each of these is to be set under the same precepts of "what a goal is" established above.

Once again, the breakout teams are reorganized and leave for their separate determinations. When done, they return to the planning room and post the lists they have developed. The leader once more guides the reconciliation of the separate lists.

The result of the reconciliation is a listing of *tentative* goals. *All* conclusions within the first planning session are considered tentative, because they must be validated before a company should be willing to bet the store. This to be accomplished during the intersession soon to be set.

There is seen on the single sheet now posted on the wall, and on the replications to be made and distributed by the traffic cop for binder inclusion, the *tentative* goals to be achieved. All goals are to be achieved not later than the third year of the plan.

An example of a goal listing follows on the next page.

GOALS TO BE ACHIEVED OVER THREE YEAR PLAN PERIOD

Overall:

Achieve $_____ in sales volume at an operatiprofit of___%.

Component Goal One:

Achieve $8MM sales of Product A in Pacific Rim market.

Component Goal Two:

Cut material loss rate at Onondaga plant from ___ % to ___ %.

Component Goal Three:

Improve productivity of Southwest region sales force from $_____ per individual to $ _____ .

D. The Planning Gap

The planning gap is defined by *the difference between what could be expected to happen in terms and revenue and earnings if no strategic plan were put in place, and what is expected to happen when one is.*

The process leader charts the differences in results between plan and no plan on two flip charts standing side by side, labeled before and after, graphically to illustrate the gap.

▶ *How to close the gap is the essence of the strategic plan.*

To this point the team has expended substantial effort, but still has not begun any plotting. It is positioned now to progress to the core of strategic planning: the strategies themselves.

SUMMARY OF SECTION THREE ACTIVITY

The planning team has established:

1. **A tentative vision expression**

2. **A tentative overall goal**

3. **Tentative ancillary goals in support of the   overall goal**

SUMMARY OF ALL PART I ACTIVITY

The following elements have been addressed:

1. *Preliminaries* – **the process protocol has been completed.**

2. *Determining Where the Company Stands Now* **has been done.**

3. *The Company's Ambitions* **have been expressed.**

4. *Tentative Vision Expression and Goals* **are in place.**

PART II

COMPLETING PLAN GENERATION

HOW THE COMPANY IS TO REALIZE ITS AMBITIONS

A. Formulating Strategy

The structure of strategic planning is:

VISION EXPRESSION

Enunciation of the overall intent of what the company is intended to be

GOALS

The specific goals that define the ambitions of the company

STRATEGY

The overall and subsidiary general paths the company will follow to achieve its goals

---

A strategy describes the general path to be followed to achieve a particular goal. It does not specify how it is to be executed, or even if that is possible. But there must be concept before there can be action.

Strategies are pithy statements, like:

- enter the market west of the Rockies
- offer new products
- manage organic growth
- pursue innovative customer initiatives
- block out the competition
- enhance operational efficiency
- improve structural effectiveness
- maximize public visibility
- open European sales office

◆**BREAKOUT SESSION: Time allotment:**
90 minutes

Establish Strategies

The leader appoints the sub-teams. By now some of the teams will be repeats, but are much more seasoned by experience. When they are in their private places their task is twofold:

1. To review the overall strategic intent determined to be extant in the Phase One sessions, and decide if it can be continued as the company moves forward, or must be replaced. If the latter, what is overall strategy to be?

2. To devise for each goal adopted at least one strategy, or as many strategies as it will take to achieve the goal.

Engagement is now heavyweight. The byword is one word tripled: creativity, creativity, creativity! The teams are to stretch and devise, innovate, invent, consider the radical. If the company has sold always through manufacturers' reps, should it put a direct sales force in place? If boldness is required to enter a new market, what way of doing it will stand the market on its head? Should the company abolish its service centers in favor of contract service organizations?

On return to the planning room the sub-teams do as expected: they post the fruits of their labors on flip chart sheets, turning over as many sheets on the pads as required. If there were three teams, for example, each of them working on four goals, with one or several strategies to be adopted for each, the front of the room becomes a busy place. The leader exerts logistic influence.

Once the sheets are completed, the leader moderates a comparison of the presentations, one goal at a time, one strategy at a time (each evaluated for conformance to the overall strategic intent asserted). The team as a whole reduces to a single reconciliation each of the goal/strategy combinations developed.

The output of the strategy session is:

Affirmation of the *tentative* strategies under which the goals adopted, *themselves still tentative*, are to be realized.

ACTION PLANS

The specific sets of actions the company will take to carry out the strategies to achieve the goals.

The structure of the process, it is seen, is a quite simple reflection of logic, a restatement of "where the company wants to go and how it is to get there." There is no great intellectual demand in understanding the concept. The challenge is to develop each element of the logic in a superior way that legitimately engenders belief that the result will obtain *advantage over the competition.*

The term "strategy" so far has hardly been mentioned, but obviously its employment lies at the core of the strategic planning process.

B. ACTION PLANS

An action plan delineates a set of specific steps to be taken to implement a defined strategy to achieve a hard goal. An action plan must always be supported by a cost/benefit analysis.

Vision is prerequisite, goals must be set, strategies to reach these must be conceived, but the company's strategic plan *depends entirely on the effectiveness of its action plans.* NOTHING ELSE COUNTS! In fact, if the company could jump immediately to a set of action plans that would achieve the company's aspirations, none of the preliminaries would be necessary. It is unlikely, however, that, without establishing the planning platform as has been done prior to this point, instinct alone could produce such a set.

♦**BREAKOUT SESSION: Time allotment:**
90 minutes

Establish Action Plan Titles

The protocol changes now. Sub-teams are not formed. Instead, participants buddy-up in pairs. The leader and chief executive promote balance in these wherein the most experienced are teamed with the lesser experienced, and functional responsibilities are mixed, once again to maximize cross-pollenization.

The instruction, before each pair finds a place to go off to, is:

For each strategy tentatively established for each goal, the pairs propose only the title of the action plan or several action plans deemed necessary to assure achievement of the goal. The reason for this is that once proper titles can be decided upon the building of the action plans themselves is facilitated.

CAUTION: Do not confuse action plans with tasks. The insurance that an action plan title is bona fide is that, just as does a bona fide goal, it has a dimension and expresses a result.

This is an action plan title:

Increase the sales force in the Southern region from three to six to achieve sales of $ _____ in 2014.

This is *not* an action plan title:

Enlarge the sales force.

Examples of good action plan titles are:

Implement methods improvement program at Bloomington facility to increase productivity from $90,000/employee to $105,000.

Introduce product line A to the EU market to achieve sales of $_____ by third year of plan period.

Improve public perception and investor communications effort to contribute to achieving stock valuation of _x_ times 12-month earnings forecast, and average daily trading volume of _____ (000) shares.

Cut average cycle time from order receipt to ship date on Class G products from four days to two.

Examples of unacceptable titles are:

Introduce an automatic pretzel maker.

Install an improved incentive program.

Straighten out the mess in the Chattanooga warehouse.

Typically, enunciations like those immediately above describe not action plans, but <u>steps</u> or tasks within a plan. Directions on how action plans are constructed is about to be illustrated.

The sub-teams return to the planning room. Extensive posting now takes place. The process leader maintains order and much wall space is likely used because the teams now require a separate sheet, or sheets, for listing action plans under each strategy supporting each goal.

The process leader reviews the postings systematically. Almost surely he or she will discover titles which are not valid titles. These must either be converted into proper titles or eliminated altogether, perhaps to reappear later as steps with action plans.

Next, evaluation by the planning team as a whole of what is on view is initiated. Considerable debate is the likelihood. While the process leader continues to moderate as to form, the chief executive asserts his or her role, and sometimes must make a ruling. We have said: strategic planning is the prime responsibility of the chief executive and it cannot be delegated. The team's function is to assist the chief executive in the adoptions to be made. Likely ideas on what the action plans should be pursued will vary widely. The chief executive considers the opinions proffered, but *alone* must make the final decision on which of the plan titles presented is to be pursued to formulation.

After the free discussion, the selections and reductions to a single listing under each strategy are made, as approved by the chief executive.

The output of the breakout session is:

A listing of the titles of action plans to be completed in definitive detail.

♦ MODELING SESSION:

The determining judgment on the adequacy of an action plan is how it demonstrates likelihood to gain advantage over the competition. That's a

challenging standard to meet, but such is the essence of what strategic planning is about.

Each action plan must have an explicit, measurable purpose, expressed in its title, e.g.:

- *Achieve profitable sales of $ _____ MM in second plan year via entering new market Y with current product A.*

- *Reduce cost of goods by ___% in (year) by installing automated equipment on line 4.*

Only occasionally, among a set of action plans which supports a strategy, is a title without dimension - but whose intent and value otherwise is clear - acceptable. (► See appendix, item D, for understanding of these incidences.)

For each action plan a leader is designated. He or she has overall responsibility for execution, but responsibility for each step within the plan must also be designated. Such appointment can be made final only after the leader <u>negotiates</u> the commitment of individuals named but not members of the full planning team; an assignment beyond the willingness of the individual to accept it cannot be made.

The leader appointed for any action plan, in side conference with individuals in the room who are likely to be designated for steps within the plan, takes a first cut at developing the action plan steps believed necessary. A definitive plan, however, can be formulated only with all individuals to be involved. Any plans tentatively developed in the planning room, however, are posted on flip chart sheets.

Sub Action Plans

Sometimes steps within a major action plan require subsidiary action plans. The requirements for these are the same as for the principal action plan.

No Planning to Plan

We do not plan to plan! An action plan step cannot be "study the market," followed by, "determine method of approach". Such tasks have to be completed *before* an action plan can be formulated. Action plans within the strategic plan presuppose essential study has been done and required data gathered. This does not mean a company should not pursue investigations on an ongoing basis - quite the contrary - but if results cannot be made available before the strategic plan is put to bed, a legitimate action plan cannot be formulated. Fruits expected from research in the future are utilized in future plans. The essence of a current action plan is that it establishes concrete, non-ambiguous steps <u>to be initiated</u> <u>now</u>.

Action Step Quality

Steps within action plans themselves specify dimensions as far as is practicable, e.g.:

Good:

"Add new salesperson in Florida territory by March 1 of the current year, to be trained by June 30, and expected to perform at 30% productivity in the third quarte,r and 60% in the fourth".

Poor:

"Add new sales person in Florida.

The Cost/Benefit Analysis

This analysis compares all costs to be incurred with the value of the specific benefit to be received from the action plan. It is based on the most realistic information that can be gathered *and will be vouched for* by the action plan leader. Be careful to define the primary assumptions on which achieving the benefit sought depends. Typical would be assessments of pricing, quality level, competitive response, development time, capital availability, cost of capital.

Usually, dollar benefits can be expressed in conventional accounting terms, like gross margin or direct expense reduction. *The benefit of sales increases is <u>always</u> expressed as the gain in gross margin, in percentage increase or total.* In some instances, however, an imputed, or judgment, value has to be used. (For instance: if a plan action was expected to reduce time required for a task by two days, the savings (or benefit) of the plan can be calculated as the people (and sometimes other) costs of the two days saved. Such savings, of course, would not show up directly as an accounting figure because the two days would be utilized otherwise. The benefit, rather, is in increased productivity, the sum of which kinds of benefits do indeed become reflected directly in reduced payroll expense. It is perfectly proper, and necessary, for a professional manager to assign a discrete dollar value to, say, the effect of advertising and sales promotion; otherwise, how is the expenditure justifiable? The trick, naturally, is <u>not to self-delude</u>.

C. ACTION PLAN MODEL

MODELING SESSION

The process leader now leads the full team in the construction of *two*, real-world, model action plans complete with their cost/benefit analyses. Suggestions on the candidates for these are taken from the floor. Any plan title can be modeled but usually some favorites will pop out of the assemblage and be selected by the process leader.

For each of the two selections decided upon for modeling, the process leader calls upon the individual designated as the action plan leader. That individual comes to the flip charts at the front of the room and constructs the model from self- and team input, and also takes suggestions from the assemblage.

The form on the next three pages illustrates the kind to be used in the development of all plans to come. It may, of course, be adapted in design to whatever arrangement is most serviceable for an individual company.

ACTION PLAN NO. ____

Title _____ **Date** _____

Leader _____

Purpose (if not implicit or explicit in the title)

_____

_____

Strategy Supported

_____

_____

Goal Supported

_____

Steps:

Overall Start Date _____

Overall Finish Date _____

Step No.	Action	By Whom	By When
1			
2			
3.			
4.			
etc.			

(As many pages as required.)

(page 1 of 3)

COST/BENEFIT ANALYSIS

A. Estimated Total Dollar Value of Benefits From Action Plan

<u>Year One</u>	<u>Year Two</u>	<u>Year Three</u>	<u>Total</u>
$000	000	000	000

B. Costs To Be Incurred:

a. Staffing

<u>Year One</u>	<u>Year Two</u>	<u>Year Three</u>	<u>Total</u>
$000	000	000	000

b. Item y

<u>Year One</u>	<u>Year Two</u>	<u>Year Three</u>	<u>Total</u>
$000	000	000	000

c. Item z

<u>Year One</u>	<u>Year Two</u>	<u>Year Three</u>	<u>Total</u>
$000	000	000	000

etc.

<u>Total Of All Costs To Be Incurred</u>

<u>Year One</u>	<u>Year Two</u>	<u>Year Three</u>	<u>Total</u>
$000	000	000	000

(page 2 of 3)

C. Net Benefit

Year One	Year Two	Year Three	Total
$000	000	000	000

Capital Expenditures

Year One	Year Two	Year Three	Total
$000	000	000	000

Assumptions And Rationale For This Action Plan:

(A succinct narrative recital)

Risks In Implementing Or Not Implementing This Plan:

(A succinct narrative recital)

During the action plan modeling exercise much of the information required, of course, can only be estimated or guessed at, but by the time the second modeling exercise is completed the planning team will have grasped how to do it when definitive plan building begins after the first planning session is completed.

PLUS:

C. Qualitative Benefits To Be Realized (In descending order of importance):

1.

2.

3.

(include for each the rationale and any dollar value also assigned)

(page 3 of 3)

D. Setting The Ongoing Schedule

The last task before adjournment of the first planning sessions is to set the schedule for plan completion. By now the team will have gained a good feel for what is required and should be able easily to arrange the calendar for the following, so:

1. **Validate the Vision Expression.**

   Validation as used here means to review the tentative expression developed, revise it as required, and convert it to the final form to which commitment will be made.

   Completion date ___ (within 7 working days)

2. **Validate tentative <u>goals</u>.**

   Completion date ___ (within 7 working days)

3. **Validate tentative <u>strategies</u>.**

   Completion date ___ (within 7 working days)

4. **Validate tentative <u>action plan titles</u>.**

   Completion date ___ (within 7 working days)

5. **Confirm INTERSESSION PERIOD.**

   Usually 60 days, commencing the day following the adjournment of the first plenary sessions.

6. **Set date for brief meeting to confirm validations.**

   Date set ___ (the last day of the period allowed for items 1.through 4.)

7. Complete all <u>product/market matrix boxes</u>.

Completion date ___ (within 20 working days)

8. Complete all items on to-do list.

Completion date ___ (within 15 working days)

9. Set date for mid-intersession review.

Date set ___ (within 20 working days)

10. Complete *all* action plans.

Completion date ___ (within 30 working days)

11. Disseminate completed action plans to all team members.

Completion date ___ (within 35 working days)

12. Establish two day final session dates.

Dates set for _____

SUMMARY OF PART II ACTIVITY

The planning team has:

1. Established tentative strategies by which to achieve the company's goals.

2. Proposed a set of action plan titles by which the company will reach its goals

3. Modeled how action plans are to be constructed and financially justified.

4. Set the schedule for a MID-INTERSESSION MEETING during which the last checkpoints are made prior to completion and presentation of the plan.

INTERSESSION

A. The Work To Be Done

Time Allotment: 60 days

If there were any doubts previously, the planning team is now aware of the scope of the effort required to generate a meaningful strategic plan. While surely there were challenging elements during the opening session, it is much more demanding to do the hard work of definitive plan formation than was the essentially drawing-room mode of the first sessions.

The completions to be made during the sixty days of intersession effort were defined by the schedule established at the end of the opening planning sessions.

In the intersession effort, the counsels to the planning team are:

1. The banner under which the process proceeds is: the strategic plan will represent, not speculation and admirable ideas, but *what the company is going to do!* The intersession period is the time during which any doubts any individual, may have, any reservations, any discomfort, any queasiness, must be resolved. The charge, in assuming the mindset of a chief executive, is effectively to communicate the basis for any questioning, then to offer convincing alternates or else fully to commit to what is adopted.

2. TIME WILL EAT YOU UP! Due dates are coming at the team rapidly. Each member is going to feel urgency and squeezing all through the rest of the process.

3. The chief executive, the process leader, and the participants are to make sure they meet, talk and otherwise communicate continuously with each other – singly, in small groups, or as a whole as seems beneficial - to make sure the work is going forward on an ongoing basis

as a team of the whole.

4. Most of the first session was outline, modeling or tentative proposition. Now all elements have to be hardened. At the same time quality must be striven for in the selections, decisions and action steps to be firmed.

▶ MID-INTERSESSION MEETING – A date is set for whole-team review of progress at the midpoint of the intersession

5. *Creativity! Creativity! Creativity!* What makes a strategic plan strategic is the stretch represented. Torture the axes of freedom wherein the strategic opportunities lie. The judgment the team will put on itself at the conclusion of planning is how honestly it believes, and can demonstrate, that each separate action to be taken will contribute to positioning the company in a way superior to any course competitors might take. As thought is given to the ideas put on the table by the team members, consider what other courses might be entertained. Are there special niches that can be addressed to particular advantage? What is worth pushing for, what not?

6. Remember: Action plans, which must be clean and complete for the scheduled concluding session are to be presented as *promises of delivery*.

7. There must be *enough* action plans, of sufficient quality, to assure goal achievement. The sum result of plans directed to each goal and to the overall goal should actually suggest overshooting the mark.

8. Be diligent in devising plans in areas critical to supporting the main-thrust plans.

9. Hard copy of each plan, together with its cost/benefit analysis, must be in the hands of all planning team members at least five working days prior the commencement of the final planning session to come. It is

useful, if any action plans are in fact completed by the time of the intersession review meeting, that they be reviewed there.

10. Uniformity in plan construction is sought not for form's sake but to facilitate digesting the material when it is presented at the final session, and reviewability as the execution phase is moved into.

11. Diligence is to be applied in the cost/benefit analyses, *a part of the regimen from which planners have been known to shrink*. Extensive, formal, financial analysis is not sought, but rather a succinct picture of bang for the buck.

Make sure only incremental benefit is counted, not any part that would have been realized without the action plan. Sometimes additional expenses to support an action plan may, or must, appear in another plan, or within a function other than the team member's. The traffic cop, process leader and chief executive, will make sure these incidences are taken cognizance of in the valuation of plans.

If, as is proper, a judgment value is assigned to a benefit not otherwise calculable, be sure that the thought processes by which the value was arrived at can be explicated.

12. Keep clear the distinction between program management and action plans. Programs are essentially schedules. Action plans are schedules too, but more especially they convey ambition, vitality and confrontation.

13. Visibility will be facilitated if each action plan author highlights key points on the hard copies to be distributed, again days before the commencement of the final session.

14. Some action plans will, naturally, promise more benefit than others. For each individual planning team member, or any other personnel asked to participate, the question is simply: what is the maximum contribution *I* can make within *my* functional responsibility or in support of the plans of others

B. Mid-Intersession Monitoring

1. At the Mid-Intersession Meeting the process leader, the entire planning team and the chief executive examine, debate for the last time, and finally approve fully validated statements of:

> **a. The Vision Expression**
> **b. Overall Goal**
> **c. Supporting Goals**
> **d. Strategies**

2. Some action plans may be ready for review at the Mid-Intersession Meeting. If so, they are presented and critiqued as they will be at the final planning session. Not infrequently plans seen at this stage are a mix of "almost there" and "a way to go." Admonition is made to button them up and eliminate deficiencies before presentation at the final planning session.

3. Verification is made that the product/market analyses now due have been completed. If such is not the case for any particular box analysis, stringent requirement for an early finish date is imposed.

4. Special Note: The concordance of action plans with product/market analyses is sometimes defective. Some plans cannot be completed until pertinent analyses are completed. The analyses may even change what was believed to be possible in a plan. Resolution of difficulties that may arise out of this factor is to be achieved at the meeting.

5. Finally, the process leader seeks identification of any element of the plan where uncertainty, laggard progress, deficient cooperation and any other impediment may be operative. The team resolves the issues, or if the chief executive must be called upon to decide ant point in contest, he or she does so.

6. <u>The Mid-Intersession Meeting is the last time the team will be together as a whole before the final planning session. All loose ends, therefore, must be attended to.</u>

7. Thoughout the intersession period the process leader, in conjunction with the traffic cop, assures ongoing adherence to protocol. Most especially, in the period following the mid-intersession meeting, the leader pays close attention to the completion of action plans and that copies of finished plans are distributed to all members on time, that is, at least five days prior to the first day of final planning session.

8. Confirm the dates on the two-day planning session.

PLAN COMPLETION

The final first-phase planning session requires one-and-a-half to two days. Only seldom can the work be completed in one day without rushing, unless a very uncomplicated set of issues and influences are the case. Once again it is desirable, but less necessary, that this session be held off-site.

The business of the final planning session is to:

1. Review and approve all action plans.
2. Confirm that all issues have been resolved.
3. Establish the plan publish date

The content of the session follows.

A. Action Plan Presentation

The schedule calls for distribution of the action plans to the planning team members at least five days before the final planning session, so that the participants are not seeing them for the first time and have a chance to digest at least their general content.

At the working session begins the process leader calls on each action plan leader, in turn, to present his or her plan. The team members offer critique, suggest modifications or sending the plan back to the drawing board. If the action plan is fully in order as presented or modified on the spot, consensus approval is given. ALL final approvals must be made by the chief executive.

Guidelines are:

1. The mode of presentation of action plans is for each leader to "sell" the plan, or plans, not simply to recite the steps. The audience will want to hear enough detail fully to understand and evaluate the likelihood of success, but it is not necessary to dwell on each line in the plan.

2. Evidence of reach, innovation, imagination and inventiveness is to be be seen.

3. "Creativity, creativity, creativity!" has already been embraced. Add to it now: Refine, refine, refine!

4. The presenter will be sure to accent orally the same key points he has highlighted on the plan copies in the hands of all team members.

5. Team leaders put themselves in a "show-off" stance wherein each expects the whole of the team to be awed by what is presented. The sum of showings-off is what will enable the company as a whole to show off.

6. Presenters are free to make changes on the fly as adrenaline, or suggestions from the floor, prompt.

B. Action Plan Approval

1. The judgment of an action plan is not just that it is logical and seems sound, but that it gives promise of doing what it purports to do in a way superior to what it is presumed the competition might do.

2. For each plan the question is posed, *"Do we believe the plan is valid and will be executed in contribution to achieving the goal it supports, on time?"* Obviously the

company is not in its strategic plan looking for adventures with low probability of success, or for rank crap shoots.

3. The house as a whole and the chief executive in particular asks:

a. Do we have enough plans to assure reaching each goal and the overall goal?

If the answer is not in the affirmative, more plans are needed.

b. Is each plan at a quality level high enough to engender confidence that its individual purpose will be achieved?

If not, the level of any defective plan must be raised.

4. Editing stops, once the approval of the chief executive is given.

C. Issue Resolution

As the moment of plan completion nears the final cross-checks are made before it can be put to bed. The process leader queries that all the issues identified in the course plan pursuit indeed have been addressed.

The leader refers the team to its planning binders wherein discrepancies between how well the company has performed and how important it is deemed by the managers have been marked as possible ISSUES. Likewise, ISSUES uncovered in probing the address to the obstacles and opportunities, and in any other component of the proceedings, and so marked in the replicas of flip charts contained in the binders, are now reviewed.

The leader goes down the ISSUES marked and asks:

a. Is the item still considered an ISSUE?

b. If so, has it satisfactorily been addressed within the plans approved for adoption?

c. If not, must the item be addressed within this planning cycle?

d. How, then, specifically is the item to be attended to? Via additional steps within the plan? By another action plan?

The results of the probing of ISSUES may be anything. They may say:

i. All issues have been addressed

ii. A few issues have not been addressed and the course to correct this has been decided upon.

iii. Decision is made that yet unaddressed issues can be ignored without affecting goal achievement.

D. Establish The Protocol For Reviewing Plan Execution

Under the process leaders guidance, the team sets the schedule for review of execution progress, so:

a. The full team meets monthly throughout the life of the plan, beginning the second month after plan publication, for on-premises review of achievement against plan at the point in time. Best practice is to schedule the review date about five days after monthly and year-to-date operating results are available.

b. The team sets the date for the Annual Plan Update review to begin, in a process analogous to the initial planning effort, sixty days prior to the anniversary date of plan publication. Strategic planning, then, is a continuous process.

E. Process Output

The planning team - therefore the company -- is now positioned to put into hard copy form:

♦ Its written strategic plan, with finite goals representing dimensional change to be achieved within a specified time frame.

♦ A prescription therein for execution to which commitment has been made.

♦ Hard establishment of the value of the gains to be achieved.

♦ A review system for assuring implementation is kept on track

F. Publishing The Plan

Finally the moment of glory has arrived. The plan is ready to be put to bed.

1. Someone writes the plan document but the authors are every member of the planning team. The process leader is an appropriate choice to do the task, but any team member, perhaps one with a taste for expository writing, may be appointed.

2. The plan proper is a simple document, perhaps of less than a dozen pages, easy to remember, easy to be referred to. It is backed up, of course, by full documentation, but the tight focus of the main document is always readily at hand.

3. The content of the summary document is:

    a. **Title Page - one page, showing:**

(Company name) Strategic Plan,   Years 20__ to 20__.
Date of publication _____
Authors (all team members, named individually)

_____

_____

_____

_____

b. Vision Expression - one page.

c. Position Statement - one page or two:

A succinct statement, authored by the chief executive, of where the company stands as the plan period begins, where it is expected to be at the end of the period, the strategic thrust it will employ to reach its overall and supporting goals.

d. Goals and Strategies - one page:

A list of overall and supporting goals and, under each, the strategies to be used in achieving each.

e. Action Plan Titles - one page or two:

Action plan titles listed under the goals they support.

▶ Alternately, the content of pages d. and e. as shown on the Strategic Plan Summary Chart, illustrated under item 7. below, will suffice.

f. Review and Update Schedule - one page:

See 5. below

g. The Action Plans - As many pages as required:

The complete set of action plans.

h. Staffing Chart - one page:

A chart of principal staffing as it stands as the plan period commences, and what it is expected to be at the end of the third year of the plan.

i. Pro-Forma Profit/Loss Statement - one page:

Prepared by the financial function head, a chart of operating performance expected in each of the three plan years.

j. Capital Spending Schedule - one page

A chart of capital expenditures anticipated to be required to support plan implementation.

4. Set the plan publish date. Although ideally the plan might be able to be written within a few days after the conclusion of the final planning session, more usually about ten working days will be required to accommodate late revisions, financial documentation and last minute negotiations. The team now commits to a publication date, upon which distribution to all team members will be effectuated.

5. The Revue and Update Schedule referenced in f. above is set by the team as follows:

- the team will review performance against strategic plan once a month. The reviews may be appended to monthly operating reviews already the custom in the company, or scheduled separately. In whichever case the dates are set down. The context of the strategic review is separate because a number of efforts will be going on which would not be addressed in the regular operating reviews.

- the first review date is to be in the second month after the plan is published. This applies whether or not the first year of the plan period has commenced or not, because <u>all actions are initiated right away</u> though their fruition dates may be some time off.

- the update is the time when the whole planning process is repeated in streamlined form. It is established as specific dates for a one-and-a-half to two day first session and, thirty days later, a one-day wrap-up session.

6. The plan writer keeps in mind that good syntax, orthography and graphic quality are to be striven for, in expression of care and pride, but also against occasions when choice might be made to show part or all of the plan outside the company walls (e.g., when a partnering arrangement is under consideration, or a merger or acquisition.) The company wants always to "look good."

7. It is useful for crystallization to include a page, as referenced in item e. above, which represents the plan essentials in chart form as follows next:

STRATEGIC PLAN SUMMARY CHART

Vision Expression - *(state it)*

Overall Goal - *(state it)*

Supporting Goals - *(state them)*

| Goal 1 | Coal 2 | Goal 3 | Goal 4 |

Strategies Supporting - *(state them by goal)*

| Goal 1 | Coal 2 | Goal 3 | Goal 4 |
| _____ | _____ | _____ | _____ |

etc.

Action Plan Titles Supporting - *(state them by goal)*

| Goal 1 | Coal 2 | Goal 3 | Goal 4 |
| _____ | _____ | _____ | _____ |

etc.

PART III

EXECUTING THE STRATEGIC PLAN

A. The Discipline Of Plan Execution

A strategic plan is a complete waste of time if it does not produce substantial result. The plan will not execute itself. If there is diligence in execution, the likelihood of success is great. If the opposite pertains a failed strategic plan is a certainty.

The bad news is: carrying through the discipline of plan realization is magnitudes more difficult than plan development.

The process leader and traffic cop will continue their roles during plan implementation, but what is most required is constant reinforcement by the chief executive that _the plan is what we are going to do,_ and managers will be judged by their commitment to making it work.

B. Mechanics Of Plan Execution

At each review meeting, moderated by the process leader, goals are reviewed in order, so:

1. Action plan leaders rise and report. Their reports can say only:

Plan on course	*or*	*Not on course*
Steps followed	*or*	*Not followed*
Steps effective	*or*	*Not effective*
Assumptions valid	*or*	*Not valid*

- or some mix of these.

2. Each report is followed by assertion that:

The end purpose of the action plan will be achieved, <u>on schedule</u>.

- or

Achievement is in doubt, but steps that have been taken either to:

a. *Rectify deficiencies.*
b. *Substitute a new plan to be submitted for team approval.*
c. *Propose a rationale for abandoning the particular action plan altogether.*

The key to meaningful reporting of action plan progress is that the steps within the plan were, or are being, executed not just on time but with qualitative excellence.

When an action plan is on target there is no need for explication. We accept that if a manager says something is so, it *is* so. If that were not true question might be raised if the individual is of manager caliber. This means that, if an action plan leader were able to recite in 15 seconds – literally that – that the plan steps were being followed with diligence and the end purpose will be achieved, nothing more need be said.

C. Adaptation

At the early scheduled review points, it is likely a number of plans will be able smartly to be reported within the fifteen-second time frame alluded to in B. just above.

At subsequent review points down the road, however, less assuring circumstances may come into focus. In that case:

1. Surprises are anathema. Meaning, if a plan is off course, the course correction and adaptations to be made are presented on the spot, but GOALS ARE NEVER GIVEN UP ON!

2. If any plan element is reported off course for any reason, or promise cannot be made that the specific purpose of the plan will be achieved, the *corrections* to be made are enunciated immediately.

3. When a plan is not on target the concentration is light on rationalization of why, but heavy on convincing presentation that the modifications to be made will be effective. Or, if the evidence is that the *assumptions on which the plan was based are wrong, or the steps poorly chosen*, there is no hesitation in offering an heavily revised or entirely new plan. Repeating: GOALS ARE NEVER GIVE UP ON!

4. After the first three review meetings, say, when a crisp routine has been established, good practice is to schedule perhaps two action plans per meeting to be reviewed in depth by the plan leaders, further to reinforce confidence.

5. Finally, for the strategic plan to work it has to be "live" in everyone's consciousness all the time. It would be major transgression for any manager not to stay with the plan continuously and to come into a review meeting unprepared

PART IV

THE ANNUAL UPDATE

How long does the strategic planning process go on?

The answer is: *Forever*!

The interpretation to be made of this assertion is that the process is self-renewing via the annual update. The update is, in effect, a repeat of the original process, but because much groundwork has already been accomplished and the team, of course, has advanced in experience, it can be completed at less expenditure of time. It is <u>not</u> at all a mechanical event, however, because new demands, new ambitions, changed conditions have to be addressed just as in the original process. These sometimes will require as much, or more, depth in probing and original thought, as did the first experience.

A. Update Preliminaries

1. In effect the update is a mini-version of the original planning sessions.

Ten working days before the first update session (as set in D., b., re protocol, above) the process leader sends questionnaires to the team members. There is asked in these:

   a. Is the plan as a whole serving the organization well? Comment on good and less good elements as you see them.

   b. In respect to plans in which you are personally involved (name them), how well-constructed have they proven to be? Has or will each plan be completed on time to satisfactory result?

   c. Of the company's overall and supporting goals, which should be carried forward as they stand? Which should be modified?

d. What new goals, if any, should be adopted as we update?

3. The process leader makes arrangements for a first update meeting, off-site, of one-and-a-half to two days and a second meeting preferably 30 days later.

B. Doing The Update

The content of the update is conversion of the existing plan, current for the three-year period whose first year is now ending, to a plan valid into the fourth year, effectively, that is, a new three year plan.

The format is:

1. An opening session of a day-and-a-half to two, rather than the two to three of the initial planning cycle.

2. A thirty-day intersession period rather than sixty.

3. No formal mid-intersession session meeting (but *ad hoc* meetings are to be held as required).

4. In most cases a single-day final session will suffice.

5. As the opening update session begins the process leader will have posted on the walls of the meeting room flip-chart sheets which display the answers to the questionnaires distributed under A., Update Preliminaries, above.

6. The team reduces the items displayed to a list of those judged now to be ISSUES. These are addressed under the prompting of the process leader with special reference to the satisfaction of stakeholders as identified in the original planning. Are there now changed, new, or as yet unsatisfied expectations?

7. Generally the leader will have to seek only quick confirmation that the Vision Expression is as durable as it was intended to be. If somehow that were not substantially true, the rework would have to be made with stern reminder that vision expressions are not to be short-lived.

8. In the manner established during the original planning session, the team reviews the principal plan elements as below. It creates from scratch only new items apprehended now to be required. Otherwise it seeks simply to refine wherever indicated the existing elements. The breakout technique is utilized freely.

♦**BREAKOUT SESSION: Time allotment:**
30 minutes

Review And Update Overall And Supporting Goals

In this, and each succeeding breakout session, again the previously well-established procedure is followed. The breakout subgroups are established and dispersed.

The charge to each is:

a. What should the overall goal for volume and operating profit be for the year beyond the original three planned for?

b. At what value should existing goals which are to be extended into the fourth year be set?

c. What entirely new goals should be established for the new plan year?

> Repeating:
>
> **GOALS ARE NEVER GIVEN UP ON!**

> If, nevertheless, any goal should, or must, be modified in some way, it is fully rationalized.

On return to the planning room the sub-teams record their conclusions on flip chart sheets posted at the front of the room.

The process leader moderates review and debate and reduces the list of altered or new goals to a single list, once again marked *tentative*.

◆BREAKOUT SESSION: Time allotment:
30 minutes

Review And Update Strategies

Shuffle sub-teams and disperse.

On return follow the familiar procedure for reduction to a single list of any new strategies *tentatively* to be included in the updated.

◆BREAKOUT SESSION: Time allotment:
45 minutes

Review And Update Action Plan Titles

Reshuffle sub-teams, disperse, return to planning room, and reduce to a single list of new or altered action plan titles.

◆BREAKOUT SESSION: Time allotment:
30 minutes

Mark The Product/Market Matrix For Current Analyses

Reshuffle sub-teams, disperse, return to planning room, reduce to a single list of "boxes" which represents:

   a. New boxes required because new products or new markets have been identified and are to be analyzed for the purpose of the updated strategic plan.

   b. Which "boxes" previously analyzed need updating for the purposes of the updated plan.

   c. Who is to analyze each of these boxes.

♦BREAKOUT SESSION: Time allotment:
                                30 minutes

Confirm *ISSUES* To Be Addressed

The breakup teams, shuffled once more and dispersed, review the ISSUES posted by the process leader and add to them any other ISSUES which have arisen in the course of the session, or are believed to be such by any team member.

On return to planning room, the ISSUES are reduced to a single list of those to be resolved within the term of the strategic plan update deliberations.

▶ At the close of the opening update session, the leader establishes with the planning team:

   1. The date for a brief meeting, not more than five days into the intersession period, to validate the goals, strategies, action plans, product/market box analyses, and issues marked to be addressed.

   2. The date for the one-day, closing update session.

C. The Update Intersession

1. The course for this is the same as the original planning intersession except that it is scheduled to be completed within 30 days rather than 60. The team members – including any new members, who are coached as they come aboard in the course of normal organizational change - are presumed to have advanced in comfort and expertise and so can be expected to work expeditiously. For the same reason of experience, a formal midpoint check meeting is usually unnecessary but may be scheduled if deemed to be useful.

If, however, any team member could offer compelling reason why somewhat more time than thirty days is required for the intersession, he or she should come forward, through the process leader to the chief executive, to request extension. This has to be done, of course, immediately as the session is to begin, or certainly not later than five working days into the period. To make such a request later than that would suggest failure to be attending to business.

2. The same counsel as for the original planning sessions obtains: members must meet, talk, exchange and otherwise communicate continuously with each other. *Ad hoc* meetings are to be called on any point that needs immediate attention.

3. The meeting to confirm validations of goals and strategies is held on time, not later than five days following the opening session.

Reminders:

THE STRATEGIC PLAN EXPRESSES WHAT THE COMPANY IS GOING TO DO!

TIME WILL EAT YOU UP!

CREATIVITY! CREATIVITY! CREATIVITY!

---

5. Hard copies of each updated or new plan, together with its cost/benefit analysis, are distributed to all planning team members at least three working days (rather than five) prior the commencement of the concluding session.

D. Completing the Updated Plan

The format is analogous to that of the original plan. In general, the final planning session will require one-and-a-half to two days, but often can be completed in a single day.

The meeting content is:

>   1. Action plan presentation
>   2. Action plan approval
>   3. Issue resolution
>   4. Setting updated-plan publish date.

E. Publish The Updated Plan

1. Appoint writer, complete documentation, distribute on the date scheduled!

2. Go forth and do good things!

APPENDIX

A. Action Plans Where Dimension Is Elusive

In the instructions on action plans in Part I, Generating The Strategic Plan, strong urging is made that an action plan must have a dimension, that is, a metric by which its success or failure can be measured. Rarely, and only then, there are issues that a company believes are vital to its interest and must be addressed with an action plan, but how to measure its result is elusive. Advertising and public relations managers are known sometimes to aver that their work can't be measured subjectively, though, of course, measuring means do exist.

The response to anyone putting forth a denial of measurement means might be: "Then what are you doing on the payroll?" Such a tweak will often spark sudden discovery of a way to assess.

Trickier still are forays into "morale" or "community relations" improvement. But even in these there is almost always a way to establish measurement standards ... and without going to the expense of practitioners, some of whose voodoo may not be more reliable than common sense or considered judgment.

Following, for instance, is the way one company attacked measurements of "leadership performance". It deemed the quality of this to be very important to achieving the company's ambitions, but did not settle for "motherhood and apple pie" statements of noble intention, nor did it expect measurement to be in terms of self-congratulatory pats on the back.

Instead it chose to measure performance in leadership on a scale of six levels as follows:

(▶ *It is easily discernible from this example that next to never can a performance measurement system not be devised.*)

LEVEL ONE: **MASTERY**

Measure Of Success:

100% OF EMPLOYEES ENGAGED

Characteristics of engagement:

- The customer is "caressed. Mutual respect for each other's value is realized.

- Clarity and unity in shared vision of what to be and how to get there.

- Relentless dialogue about improving personal and business performance

- Active learning as a competitive advantage

- Professionals are banging at the doors to be employed

LEVEL TWO: **OUTSTANDING**

Measure Of Success:

BETTER THAN 80% OF EMPLOYEES INVOLVED

Characteristics of engagement:

- Serving individual customers they know personally, taking full responsibility for the relationship – doing what's best.

- Contributing to strategy, plans and budgets, setting stretching (but not insane) goals. Following up frequently

- Seeking 80+ hours per year for self and personal enrichment

- Competition wants to understand employment practices and benefits.

LEVEL THREE: **SATISFACTORY**

Measure Of Success:

MOST EMPLOYEES INVOLVED

Characteristics of engagement:

- ♦ Teams working on customer satisfaction and ISO quality improvement processes.

- ♦ Communicating and achieving financial and personal performance targets.

- ♦   Attending regular training programs.

- ♦   Turnover at or below industry norm.

LEVEL FOUR: **ACCEPTABLE**

Measure Of Success:

EMPLOYESS BELIEVE IN THE FUTURE, WANT POSITIVE CHANGE

Characteristics of engagement:

- ♦ Customers assess services no better, no worse than that of others.

- ♦ Financial and planning tools are adequate – improve understanding.

- ♦ Emerging leadership potential among employees is being identified.

- ♦ Survival tactics are balanced with forward planning and investments.

LEVEL FIVE: **INTOLERABLE**

Measure Of Success:

GENERALLY GOOD PEOPLE BUT MANAGE MENT GETTING IN THE WAY

Characteristics of engagement:

- ♦ Customers try to find other outlets to fulfill service needs

- ♦ Top down direction is primary form of communication.

- ♦ Financial information is guarded and held by few personnel.

- ♦ Work force is dependent rather than loyal.

LEVEL SIX: **CRASH**

Measure Of Success:

TOTAL LACK OF LEADERSHIP

Characteristics of engagement:

- ♦ Frustrated customers become vigilant and seek out competitors

- ♦ Financials considered not worth reporting

- ♦ Work force has an "it's a paycheck" attitude.

- ♦ Emerging leaders are long gone.

- ♦ Customers try to find other outlets to fulfill service needs

B. The Origins Of Strategic Planning

For the historically disposed, it can be noted that in every decade this or that theorist proposes an astounding new approach. It is quickly evident that the only new feature seen in the proposals is newly-coined vocabulary and jargon. The proponent might even dare to suggest a revolutionary concept. Nonsense! The truth is, nothing has changed since the foundress formalized the discipline centuries ago.

The foundress, or at least she could be called that, is Diane de Poitiers, a mistress of Henry II in sixteenth century France. Henry, in the good days, gifted her with large but minimally productive estates. Diane was wise enough to understand that the tenure of mistresses is uncertain and, knowing that a girl has to provide for herself, she set about a process of genuine strategic planning and execution wherein she assessed what she possessed, determined creatively how the holdings could be utilized for maximum return, and resolutely followed through on the course adopted. This is not to say that others before Diane had not acted similarly, but the documentation of how she proceeded is prime evidence that there is very little new in earthly endeavors, and neat indication of how little attention habitually is paid to the past.

▶ **Lesson: Pay attention to the logic of the methodology here contained.**

C. The Author

Prior to devoting his talents to catalyzing strategic plotting as Managing Partner of ADG Strategy Catalysts, Charles Cherry served in CEO and other senior management roles in high-tech, industrial, and consumer product companies. He was President of Universal Laboratories and Executive Vice President at Hooker-American. For the Columbian Group he was President of Coradi AG in Europe. Earlier in his career he advanced through a variety of marketing and division management assignments at Fairchild and Sybron.

Mr. Cherry has worked with companies in diverse fields, in both the U.S. and Europe, among them: energy and access control systems; fasteners; telecommunications; medical instrumentation; computer components, peripherals and software; precision mechanical components; laser optics; rate analysis services; engineering services; gas detection analyzers; military avionics; lubricants; chemical specialties and specialty chemicals, ceramic materials; silicon wafers; beauty salons; retailers; advanced materials; financial services; distributors; franchises; coatings; appliances; publishing; private and university research; not-for-profit area development; boating equipment construction; chromatography; high-temperature furnaces; writing and marking instruments; freight forwarding; mass spectrometers; industrial refrigeration equipment; process controls; hospitality services, machine tools. (The key issues extant in some of these at the time of Mr. Cherry's engagement are noted in D. next.)

Some key roles Mr. Cherry has played have been in the conception and development of product firsts, in the negotiation of exclusive arrangements with foreign governments, and in overseeing the licensing and set-up of manufacturing in Europe and Latin America. His real world experiences include start-ups, turnarounds and substantial wins.

Cherry has served on the boards of directors of several companies and is a frequent speaker and published author. He studied Industrial Administration at Yale's School of Engineering and did his graduate work at Columbia.

D. A Sampling Of Issues

A sampling of the kinds of issues client companies were facing when ADG Strategy Catalysts guided them in strategy development, productivity improvement, and raising end-performance level:

Precision Mechanical Components	*Extending market coverage*
Software Developer	*Continued expansion after IPO*
Analytical Instruments	*Internationalization*
Machine Tools	*Consolidation of brand names*
Computer Peripherals	*Increasing share value*
Silicon Wafers	*German giant expanding in U.S.*
Defense Avionics	*Adapting to change*
Web Content Provider	*Integrating Asian facilities*
Chemicals	*Growth mid heavy competition*
Construction Contractor	*Coherent forward direction*
Retail Chain	*Expanding area coverage*
Telecommunications	*Compete against Big Three*
Household Appliances	*Expanding customer base*
Beauty Salon Franchisor	*Exploiting trailblazer concept*
Financial Services	*Improve target focusing*
Trucker	*Profitability in expansion mode*
Computer Components	*Executing turnaround*
Process Control Devices	*Broadening markets to be pursued*
Packaging	*Seeking breakthrough*
Ceramic Ware	*Revitalizing moribund line*
High-Tech Manufacturer	*Reduction of time to market cycle*

Scientific Instruments	Satisfying Big Board parent
Electronics Manufacturer	Time to market
University Research Foundation	Accommodating growth
Analytical Instruments	Entry into new markets
Laser Optics	Preparation for IPO
Medical Instruments	Approach to unrealized potential
Industrial Furnaces	How to move flat sales slope up
Equipment Lessor	Exploitation of unique market
Engineering Services	Profitability in strong expansion
Software Developer	Establishing niche position
Travel Services	Bringing order to agglomeration
Electronic Parts Distributor	Domination of specialty market
Gas Detection Instruments	Succession in family-ownership
Refrigeration Equipment	Market expansion
Bank	Market development
Environmental Devices	Finding niche
Area Development	Attracting enterprise location
Fashion House	Discipline in creative culture
Aerospace Instrumentation	Solidifying position

www.ingramcontent.com/pod-product-compliance
Lightning Source LLC
Chambersburg PA
CBHW081237180526
45171CB00005B/455